BOOK OF THE
CAMP FIRE GIRLS

CAMP FIRE GIRLS, Incorporated
65 Worth Street, New York, N. Y. 10013´

Cat. No. D-70
Prepared by the Division of Program Services
Camp Fire Girls, Inc.

A Letter To You

DEAR CAMP FIRE GIRL:

This is your book, written especially for you and for every girl who wants to be a Camp Fire Girl.

It tells about the wonderful times you'll have with your Camp Fire group, and with your guardian. (She's your group leader.)

Camp Fire Girls do exciting things in their group meetings, at home and out of doors too, like taking picnic hikes, cooking outdoors (and in), singing and dancing and playing games.

Sometimes they give a play or a puppet show. They like to make things, do experiments, discover new nature hobbies, and help other people. And what fun Camp Fire Girls camping will be—swimming, learning new skills and making new friends!

This is your book; use it as your guide to the fascinating activities and Camp Fire honors in the Seven Crafts. Some of the honors you'll earn at home, and others will be fun to do at your group meetings.

This book also tells you how to become a Trail Seeker and a Wood Gatherer, and how to achieve the rank of Fire Maker. (Torch Bearer rank is for older girls; their books tell all about that.)

This is the secret of Wohelo's trail—to dream, to seek, to find, to share. Be happy! Camp Fire is for you and every girl, to help you *enjoy* being a girl.

HESTER TURNER
National Executive Director

P.S. Please share this letter with your parents.

Foreword

This is a new book, yet it is an old book. It is for the Camp Fire Girls of today, but it keeps all the good things that have always been found in the BOOK OF THE CAMP FIRE GIRLS.

Many people have helped to make this book for you. In the Division of Program Services, Doris Foster wrote the greater part of it, and Goldie Taub Chernoff prepared the section about the "lively arts" and creative arts.

The artist who made the drawings is Marg Hartelius, and Paul Hartelius designed the book.

If you want to, you can keep your own record of the things you do and the honors you earn, right in this book; there are special pages for this. You can make this BOOK OF THE CAMP FIRE GIRLS a book of happy memories that you will want to keep always.

Division of Program Services

WHAT IS IN THIS BOOK

My name: _Jenny Bartlett_

Street: _River Road_

City and State: _Pawcatuck, Ct._

My Camp Fire name: _Makowee_

Its meaning: _Earth Maiden_

My Camp Fire group name: _____

Its meaning: _____

My symbol   **My group symbol**

WORSHIP GOD

Creation is God's gift to us; with our *hearts* we worship and praise Him.

Everything comes from God. Worship God means to honor and respect God in word and action. Serving God means respecting every person and treating him fairly, because we all belong to God.

SEEK BEAUTY

Eye and *thought* are used, because we must be able to see and appreciate beauty to find it. To seek beauty is to look for it, everywhere around you. Beauty is found in music, sunsets, snowflakes, white clouds in a blue sky, your home, stars at night, wild flowers, a baby, a soft, warm, cuddly puppy, or in the smile in the eyes of a friend. Where else do you find beauty?

GIVE SERVICE

Heart, hand and *thought* symbolize the sympathy, understanding and knowledge we need to give service.

With a loving heart and willing hands, give service to others because you want to make the lives of others a little happier.

PURSUE KNOWLEDGE

Hand and *thought* mean that to acquire knowledge we must use our skill as well as we can.

You pursue knowledge to be a better person: in understanding, in doing, and in being what you want to be. One way you pursue knowledge is to earn new honors in the Seven Crafts and achieve Camp Fire ranks.

Camp Fire Girls

BE TRUSTWORTHY

Symbols for *honesty* and *heart* are used, for the desire to be trustworthy must be rooted in our heart.

Be honest and truthful. Be fair in work and in play. It means you are worthy of trust.

HOLD ON TO HEALTH

Heart and *thought* mean that to be healthy we must live wisely.

Good health habits in eating, sleeping, cleanliness, exercise, and fresh air will mean bright cheeks, sparkling eyes, and a happy smile. Good health is a precious gift, so we do all we can to hold on to it.

GLORIFY WORK

The *hand* represents work, and *heart* represents wholehearted effort.

This means to be proud of your work and of doing it well. Sing as you help at home, at school, and at Camp Fire meetings, and it will be fun to work! You have a real share in helping others. By always trying to do your best, you "glorify work."

BE HAPPY

Heart, growth and *thought* are combined, for we must create our happiness in heart and mind.

With kind words, kind deeds, and a friendly smile, try to make other people happy. The best way to do this is to have a happy heart yourself. Catch a happy smile and put it in your pocket—never let it get away!

The Objectives of Camp Fire Girls, Inc.

As you have seen, the Law of the Camp Fire Girls has many thoughts in it about what Camp Fire Girls want to do and become. Adults belonging to Camp Fire Girls believe in this Law, too, but they express what they want for girls a little more fully, in the Objectives of Camp Fire Girls:

- high ideals to live by, day by day;
- a love of home and family that grows as you grow;
- a quiet pride in being a girl and a full measure of womanly qualities;
- deep love of your country, a knowledge of what democracy means, readiness to serve;
- many friends, and the fun and happiness of making and keeping more, all through your life;
- good health, and the habits that will help you keep it;
- the ability to take care of yourself, to do your work skillfully, and to take pleasure in it;
- interests, skills, and hobbies you can enjoy with others and alone;
- love of the out-of-doors, and skill in outdoor living;
- a happy heart that will help you find beauty, romance, and adventure in the common things of daily life.

Part 1

GETTTING STARTED IN CAMP FIRE

BECOMING A MEMBER

Welcome!

Are you new to Camp Fire Girls? Or were you a Blue Bird? Either way, something wonderful is happening to you: you are starting on the Camp Fire trail.

Being a Camp Fire Girl is special and exciting. So many adventures are waiting for you. So many Camp Fire friends are ready to share them.

Just think! You belong to a national organization with members all over the United States of America. Wherever you go, you can find Camp Fire sisters. Even if you move, your membership card can introduce you to Camp Fire friends and make you feel at home right away.

How to Join

The most important reason for joining Camp Fire Girls is wanting to belong. The only things you need to do (these are called membership requirements) are:

1. Be nine, ten, or eleven years old or in the fourth, fifth, or sixth grade.
2. Return to your guardian a membership application signed by your parents.
3. Pay your Camp Fire Girls national membership dues of $2.00.
4. Learn the Law of the Camp Fire Girls.

Then comes the moment when you stand before the other members of your group and your Camp Fire guardian, and with pride say the words of the Law of the Camp Fire Girls.

Membership Dues

Members of Camp Fire Girls, girl or adult, pay annual national membership dues of $2. (Blue Birds pay $1.) Money from dues helps Camp Fire Girls to grow. Most girls earn their dues, usually with the group, but sometimes by themselves. It is fun when the group plans ahead and earns the money together for the next year. You pay your national dues each year in the group's birthday month.

Just as in other groups, *you are a member only as long as your dues are paid.* Only registered members may earn honors and ranks. You see how important it is for you to pay your dues. Each girl receives her own membership card and the group will have its special charter showing that it is registered.

Your Guardian

Your Camp Fire group has a *guardian.* The dictionary says a guardian is "one who keeps safe." When you were a Blue Bird, your group had a *leader;* now you are a little older and can begin to learn about leadership yourself, but your guardian is there to help you do it. Sometimes groups have an assistant guardian, and every group has adult sponsors (Chapter 22 tells about sponsors).

GETTING ACQUAINTED

Getting to Know Each Other

Now you are a member; you have become a Camp Fire Girl. It is time to get acquainted. First of all, you will get to know the girls in your group. What are their names? Do they have sisters or brothers? Can you guess their favorite songs and games?

The other girls and your guardian will want to know about you, too. What do you like to do best of all? What do you do after school every day? What do you play? Do you like to go on hikes and take a picnic lunch? Do you like to make things? If you were a Blue Bird, tell about what you did in your Blue Bird group.

Getting to Know about Camp Fire

Next, all of you will want to know more about being a Camp Fire Girl.

Camp Fire Girls Symbol or Insigne—is the crossed logs and red flame inside the Wohelo triangle.

1. From early times the flame (fire) meant *home*, and *woman* was the keeper of the fire.
2. The fire also stands for the *outdoors*, the campfire, meaning beauty, wonder, and friendliness.

This stands for two very important parts of its program for girls.

Your Membership Pin—looks like the insigne shown above. It has a red flame and a red triangle outline. You may wear your pin on your Camp Fire Girls costume or at any time, to show that you are proud to be a member of Camp Fire Girls.

Camp Fire Girls Colors—are red, white, and blue. They remind us of our country.

Camp Fire Girls Watchword—is a "Camp Fire" word—Wo-he-lo. One of the founders of Camp Fire Girls, Mrs. Luther H. Gulick, made it up from the first two letters of three very important words: Work, Health, and Love. The triangle shape of the insigne was designed by her also, to remind us of these three words. The word Wohelo comes into many things in Camp Fire, in songs, in ceremonials, in the three ranks. It has deep meaning for every Camp Fire Girl.

Camp Fire Girls Slogan—is *Give Service*. It is also the third part of the Camp Fire Girls Law.

In Camp Fire you'll find many ways of giving service. How? By being thoughtful of others, happy, interested, and considerate. By finding things that you can do to make someone's day a little brighter, you may be surprised to find that your day is a little brighter, too.

Camp Fire Girls Costume— is a Camp Fire blue skirt, crisp white blouse, red Camp Fire tie. You can read more about the costume in Chapter 4.

Camp Fire Girls Symbols

Camp Fire Girls has its own special word-pictures, or symbols. Many of them are based on American Indian symbol patterns. There is symbolism all through the Camp Fire Girls program: in the Camp Fire name which you'll choose for yourself, in your group's name, in the name of the organization itself. The Camp Fire ranks and the Seven Crafts (which you'll find in Chapters 7 and 8) have symbols too.

Camp Fire Girls Seven Crafts

The Seven Crafts are general areas of interest for girls, which probably you will want to know more about as you grow up. The areas are: Home, Outdoors, Creative Arts, Citizenship, Science, Sports and Games, and Business. Can you imagine things which you might like to do, which might come under these Crafts? (Craft is an old English word that means *strength, skill,* or *knowledge.*)

Within each Craft, you will find many activities which girls choose to do in order to have fun, to try something new, or to learn more about whatever they like best. Each one of these activities is called an *honor*.

If you ever wonder "what will I do now?" just look at the list of honors under the Seven Crafts. Ideas pop up out of every line! Many you can do yourself; others are projects for you to do with your group.

Camp Fire Girls Ranks

The three ranks in Camp Fire are stepping stones along the Camp Fire trail. They are Trail Seeker, Wood Gatherer, and Fire Maker. Each one takes you further along the trail, toward growing up and liking it.

Every rank is an invitation to you to do many things: sample honors in all of the Seven Crafts, grow in service, learn new skills, and have good times aplenty in your Camp Fire group.

Girls work toward the rank of

Trail Seeker: when they are 9 years old or in the fourth grade.

Wood Gatherer: when they are 10 years old or in the fifth grade.

Fire Maker: when they are 11 years old or in the sixth grade.

Although girls progress along the Camp Fire trail in this order, a new member may begin with the rank best suited to her age or grade. This means she does not have to start with the first rank, if she is older than 9 years or beyond the fourth grade.

Each rank has its own insigne or symbol with its special meaning. You will find these in Chapter 7.

HOW CAMP FIRE GIRLS BEGAN

So many of the best stories begin, "When Grandma was a girl. . . ." That's the way the story of Camp Fire Girls begins too. There are many grandmas today who were among the first Camp Fire Girls. Is there, perhaps, a girl in your group whose grandma was a Camp Fire Girl? Then you can hear about the early days from her!

Those early days began in 1910. Certain men and women were concerned about boys and girls and the fact they had nothing much to do after school that was really interesting, or would help them to grow up to be strong and healthy and good citizens. This was at a time when mothers were beginning to have jobs, and when more and more things were being invented. Looking ahead, these men and women saw that many ways of doing things would change. People would travel faster and farther than ever before. Many new kinds of jobs would need to be filled. There would be many more things to learn.

But in spite of all the changes they saw coming, these people knew it was important to keep some things that should continue to be a part of living: things like music and singing, and dancing, and making beautiful objects with one's hands, like knowing about and loving the beauties of nature, and thinking lovely thoughts and trying to put them into words.

Early in 1910, all these ideas began to develop into plans. The first result of the planning was the Boy Scouts of America. But almost as soon as that organization appeared, questions began. What about the girls? Was there any program, any organization, designed just for girls? Certain churches did have organizations for girls. But nowhere in the country was there a program for girls of all races and national backgrounds and religious beliefs.

Very well known among this group of "idea people" was the man who, with his wife, became the founder of Camp Fire Girls—Dr. Luther Halsey Gulick. He helped begin two things that summer of 1910 which became a part of the basic program of Camp Fire Girls. One was a pageant given in the town of Thetford, Vermont. From this pageant came the name Camp Fire Girls; the original three ranks (known as Wood Gatherer, Fire Maker, Torch Bearer); the name "guardian" for the group leader; the idea of the ceremonial; and the first Camp Fire costume. Have you ever seen a picture of the girls in the long white middies and the full dark blue bloomers?

The other thing which began that summer was the program Dr. and Mrs. Gulick worked out at their camp for girls on Lake Sebago in Maine. For twenty years the Gulicks and their own four daughters and two sons had a family camp in Connecticut, and they had recently begun a girls' camp in Maine. Going off to summer camp was almost unheard of at that time, especially for girls. This was really an adventure; these girls were camping pioneers!

Anyway, seventeen excited girls (counting the three Gulick girls who were almost young ladies by this time) were the first Camp Fire Girls camp group. They were older than you are now, of course. Today girls that age would be Horizon Club girls. But they were just as new to camping as the youngest Camp Fire Girl or even Blue Bird of today.

At Camp Sebago-Wohelo they had much the same fun as you will have at Camp Fire Girls camp; swimming, canoeing, learning campcraft, taking part in council fires. The girls chose their Camp Fire names. Dr. and Mrs. Gulick had Camp Fire names, too, very well suited to them; Mrs. Gulick was Hi-i-te-ni (life-more-abundant; desire-for-attainment), and Dr. Gulick was called Ti-ma-nous (guiding spirit). The girls learned how to make and decorate their ceremonial gowns. Mrs. Gulick shared with them the knowledge she had gained from the expert on Indian lore, Ernest Thompson Seton. So the program had from the very beginning this special American touch which it still keeps as its own identifying symbolism.

By fall that year, the main points of the program were tried and liked by girls. Dr. Gulick and his group gathered more grownups who were interested in forming an organization for girls. Stories appeared in leading magazines and newspapers. Soon people all over the country were hearing about the exciting things girls could do in a Camp Fire group. The number of Camp Fire Girls groups grew very quickly. Blue Bird groups were formed in 1913, when younger girls insisted on being part of the Camp Fire Girls program too! It was a long time—1941— before Horizon Clubs for high school girls, were formed. And in 1962, the older Camp Fire Girls began to be called Junior Hi Camp Fire Girls.

Dr. Gulick said, "The keynote (of Camp Fire Girls program) is . . . our wish to develop girls to be womanly." He felt that the making of a home and the bringing up of children would always be the first duty of most women, and that women should always feel a joy and pride in giving service to the home, and also to the community. This was to be a program for girls. It was not to do things as they were done in a boys' program. Girls and boys, as they grow into women and men, have somewhat different parts to take in the world, and so their interests will differ in many ways.

Mrs. Gulick also gave Camp Fire Girls program its strong belief that it is fun to be a girl. About homemaking, for example, she said, "Woman's work . . . is far more fascinating than man's . . . it has the greatest variety. . . . We must think about it as men do about their work, to make it as interesting, and as successful." About beauty, she wrote in the very first BOOK OF THE CAMP FIRE GIRLS, "Where it (beauty) is lacking, help create it; where it is present, appreciate it. We must show it in our actions; we must see it in nature and in people, and we must love it in our hearts." And about service: "Love your neighbor, and service will be as unconscious and beautiful as the service of a father or mother, brother, sister or friend. Therefore, let us seek to establish love in our hearts; service will follow. Though not so easy, the opposite is true: serve your neighbor and love will follow."

Many men and women in your community work in the Camp Fire Girls program, to help make it possible for you to enjoy. They have the same hopes and ideals for you. In years to come, when you are grown up, you will help bring this organization to girls too! More and more thousands of girls will share in the fun and friendship. This is the way that Camp Fire Girls began. It will continue to be the way that Camp Fire Girls is handed on.

YOUR CAMP FIRE COSTUME

As a Camp Fire Girl, you have a special costume. Attractive and colorful, it looks well on every girl. You may wear it as soon as you are a member.

Your Service Costume

The Camp Fire Girls service costume is the Camp Fire blue skirt, white tailored blouse, and red Camp Fire tie. The hat is a Camp Fire blue beret. You can tell it's really Camp Fire because each part of the costume has the crossed logs and flame embroidered on it. Wear plain low-heeled shoes with your service costume. Why is it called a "service costume"? Because our slogan is Give Service.

When do you wear your Camp Fire service costume? You will wear it to your group meetings of course, and on trips with your group. Perhaps you can wear it to school during Camp Fire Girls birthday week in March each year. Wear it whenever you represent Camp Fire Girls. Always be spick and span and wear a bright, courteous Camp Fire smile!

Remember that whenever you wear your Camp Fire costume, you represent all Camp Fire Girls everywhere. Whatever you do or say, and the way you look, reflects on your organization. Be proud of your appearance as a Camp Fire Girl!

Your Ceremonial Costumes

For your Camp Fire ceremonial costume you have a choice of two styles:

1. the Camp Fire blue ceremonial jacket, worn *with* your service costume, or
2. the light brown cotton ceremonial gown with brown suede leather fringe.

Important parts of your ceremonial costume, either jacket or gown,

are the honor beads and other symbols with which you decorate it.
These make your ceremonial costume an always-growing record of
your progress on the Camp Fire trail. That is why no two ceremonial
costumes are exactly alike. (You will find both styles pictured in Chapter 9.)

You'll want to get your ceremonial jacket first, while you are working toward your Trail Seeker rank. If you are ten when you join, and
starting to become a Wood Gatherer, you'll want it as soon as possible.
Many girls also get a ceremonial gown while they are achieving Fire
Maker rank, for by this time they have many honors and much progress
to record. Others continue to decorate their ceremonial jackets. The
choice of jacket or gown is always yours. You'll wear the ceremonial
costume when you are a Junior Hi Camp Fire Girl too, and achieving
the more grown-up ranks of group and individual Torch Bearer.

The Ceremonial Jacket

You wear your ceremonial jacket and service costume at your own
group ceremonials when you receive honor beads and other awards
you have earned, and at the occasional council fire. Take it to Camp
Fire Girls camp for council fire.

But that isn't all. Showing the honors you have earned is a good way
to tell people about your good times in Camp Fire. You will also be
proud to wear your jacket in your community, on special occasions.
This might be Camp Fire Girls Day at church or synagogue, a Camp
Fire Girls program at school or at parents' meetings, or perhaps at a
United Fund rally. You might take your jacket to school and show it to
your friends.

Just remember that your ceremonial jacket is worn on *special* occasions. In a way it is a Camp Fire party dress. You wouldn't wear a
party dress to school every day, to square dance, to take part in sports,
or to do most service projects. The same is true of your ceremonial
jacket. If you think of this, you will be able to decide for yourself just
when and when not to wear your ceremonial jacket.

The Ceremonial Gown

Your ceremonial gown is even more special than your ceremonial
jacket. It is worn *only* by you, and *only* at group ceremonials and coun-

cil fires. One exception to this might be your wearing your gown on a parade float or in a pageant telling about Camp Fire Girls.

Think for a moment how personal and how beautiful a ceremonial gown is. Think how strange it would look if you wore it to a party or along the street. People wouldn't appreciate its beauty and meaning, and you wouldn't have a chance to explain it well. That is why the ceremonial gown is kept only for very special Camp Fire Girls occasions.

A Camp Fire Girl's ceremonial gown is made in the style of the lovely buckskin gown of an American Indian maiden, but it is not an "Indian costume."

Your Camp Fire Tie

Much of the neatness of your whole Camp Fire costume depends on the correct arrangement of your tie. This is how you wear it:

1. Place your tie under the collar of your blouse with the crossed logs and flame showing in the back. Tie the ends in front with a square knot, or slip them through a tie slide horizontally, as illustrated. Have the knot about 3 or 4 inches from the tip, not looking as if it would choke you under your chin! Each group usually decides whether its members will use the knot or a tie slide.

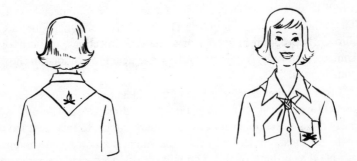

2. With your ceremonial jacket, the tie is worn *under* your collar but *over* your jacket. Again be sure your tie is neat, with the corner having the embroidered crossed logs and flame *centered* on the back of your jacket. You decorate your jacket so nothing gets in the way of this. (See the illustration.)

Why "Costume"?

You may wonder why we use the word *costume* to describe what Camp Fire Girls wear. This word does suggest something more than Halloween! It means "what people wear," especially women. Because Camp Fire Girls *is* for girls, and we are happy that it is, the people who began Camp Fire Girls chose that feminine and special word, "costume."

Where to Buy Your Costume

Ask your guardian which local store has a Camp Fire Girls outlet. If there is none, order through your Camp Fire Girls council. If your group is not in a council, then order directly from Camp Fire Girls, Inc., Supply Division, 450 Avenue of the Americas, New York, N. Y. 10011.

PLANNING YOUR MEETINGS

Democracy is our way of work and play in a Camp Fire group, as it is also in leaders' meetings where guardians plan together, and in our government.

What does democracy mean to your group? It will mean that every girl is welcome. It will also mean that every girl will have the chance to say what she thinks, and that her ideas, whatever they are, will be respected. No two snowflakes are alike; neither are any two girls. We respect and admire each girl for her good qualities.

Making a group decision is sometimes hard and sometimes easy. But it is a good way to be democratic because everyone has a chance to express her point of view before the group decides. It is a good way to be polite, too. A democratic group is considerate of everyone.

Important Things to Decide

Your group will want to discuss:

Where to meet: Will it be in a meeting room at school or church or synagogue? Or at the home of your guardian? Or at your sponsor's home sometimes? Or will you take turns meeting in the homes of the girls? Where is the best place for most of the girls? Sometimes meetings held outdoors are the most fun of all. Talk it over and decide together.

When to meet: How long will you meet? What time? Which day of the week is best for your guardian and for the girls? Make one day "Camp Fire Day" every week.

Electing your group officers:

These are officers most Camp Fire groups elect, and what they do.

President who conducts the meetings.
Vice president who takes the President's place if she must be absent.
Secretary who writes the minutes of the meetings.
Treasurer who keeps account of group dues and other money received, earned, or paid out. She gives all money to

the guardian for safekeeping, or with the guardian's help, deposits it in a bank.

Scribe   who writes up the news of special group events for the local newspaper.

All officers have the advice and help of the guardian, and all the girls help make plans and decisions. Before you hold elections, talk over what officers would do in *your* group, and how long officers would serve.

If you hold an election every six months, will all girls have a chance to be an officer during the year? How do you have an election? There are many things to talk over before you vote.

Group Funds

Think what your group will need money for this year: national membership dues, Camp Fire books, group supplies, other things you want to do. Most groups make a rule to pay dues amounting to five, ten, or fifteen cents per week. Some of these expenses can be earned by group money-making projects. Your group will vote to decide what it wants to do about this.

A Group Name

When you are ready to choose a group name, look ahead to Chapter 7. Think about what you want your group to stand for, or to do.

When the group has decided, choose a group name. This should be written in carefully on your group charter. Later you'll want to choose a symbolgram together, to show in a design what your group name means to you and to other girls.

Hints for Planning

Planning is fun! It's also easier when all the girls in the group remember these hints:

1. Give every girl a chance to express her ideas.
2. Look over the suggestions in this book—chapter headings, requirements for rank, honors in the Seven Crafts.
3. What other things would you like to do with your group? Decide on some of these.
4. Choose one or two things the group wants to do first. As a group, vote or agree on this. Then all take part.

5. Put together the ideas that are alike to make a list. (See the example below.) Keep in mind that you will always want to be adding to this list. You might start an Idea Box for the same purpose.

6. Make a calendar.

List of Ideas for Meetings—

One group might list Ideas for Meetings this way. Similar ideas, such as things to do outdoors, parties, etc., are grouped together.

OUTDOORS
- A picnic in the park
- A hike to see the sunset
- Cooking out, and learning how to camp
- A trip to the flower show or botanical gardens

SERVICE
- Sing carols at Christmas—to shut-ins, at the bus station, in our neighborhood
- Explain Camp Fire to some Blue Birds
- Plan a Camp Fire exhibit for the United Fund Drive
- Plant trees on the new school lawn

MAKING THINGS
- Puppets and scenery for a play
- Sewing for the Needlework Guild
- Painting shelves for our Camp Fire meeting room
- Something for Mother's Day

CEREMONIALS

- One with a Thanksgiving theme because we are thankful
- One to welcome our new member
- A big one where we can invite our mothers and fathers
- One to launch a service-to-others project

PARTIES

- For a foreign student or visitor in the community
- For children in the day nursery
- For us—a skating party

A Calendar

Making a calendar helps to fit your group's activities into your meeting time.

1. Rule eight large squares on 1 or 2 sheets of paper.
2. Write in your meeting days and dates for the next two to four months, so that each square stands for one meeting.
3. Take a look at your Ideas List and Idea Box. Check to see what holidays or special events fall in the months you are planning for. Look again at the requirements for rank which your group will be working on. Which month and which meeting fits best, for each big project your group definitely wants to do?
4. Use a pencil and mark in the group's ideas. (You can always change your plans later if you wish.) Try to chart your big activities. Then your group won't discover too late that there isn't time for some things you wanted to do most.
5. Now that the big events are mapped in, you'll find you want to use some of the other meetings to prepare for the big meetings, and for follow-up afterwards. At other meetings, you will use other ideas from your List. Or you may think of something else, when the time is closer. Don't worry about those empty spaces!

Meeting Day

The day of your meeting is here! How do you open the meeting? What will you do while you're there? How do you close and say "See you next week"? So many questions! Each meeting is different, very special and important.

A Camp Fire meeting is something like your favorite sandwich: the top slice is the opening. The bottom slice is the closing ceremony. The filling? That's the exciting activity your group planned for that day.

Opening

Some groups start a meeting with songs, a game or two, perhaps the Camp Fire Girls Law or one of the Desires. Some have a flag ceremony. Some ask each girl to tell about the most beautiful thing she has seen all day. Some have a roll call, answering with their Camp Fire names. Try a different opening each time.

Singing together is great fun when you know the songs. Have some singing at almost every meeting, Camp Fire songs, fun songs, camp songs, and the lovely folk songs. Old and new favorites are just waiting for you in Chapter 11. Sing those you know first. Then try new songs. You'll be earning honors too.

Games are a part of almost every meeting too. Some groups play an active game outdoors before the meeting starts, especially if the girls have been in school all day. Others have a game later in the meeting. Chapter 17 suggests many kinds of games. Do you know one you can teach your group?

Main Part

For that filling, there is whatever activity you have helped your group to plan: a hike, a service project, cooking, making things, or perhaps a group ceremonial.

Closing

After putting away and cleaning up, it's nice to close with a favorite Camp Fire ceremony, something the girls in the group have planned. It might be a candle ceremony, a friendship circle, one of the Desires, a good night song, and always a thank you for your guardian.

MONEY: YOUR GROUP'S AND YOUR OWN

Your group has exciting plans. There are things you want to do together, and group dues only go so far. You will need to earn some money for your group treasury. Camp Fire Girls are proud to pay their own way.

After your group plans what it wants to do, it will need to find out how much this will cost. Then you plan how to pay as you go.

Group Money-Earning

There are many ways a group can earn money. Each group usually has one money-earning project a year. Your guardian tells the program committee of your Camp Fire Girls council about this project.

Good Practices for Money-Earning

- Always give full value for money you receive. Make this your motto for all Camp Fire money-earning projects.
- Keep the project simple. Don't let it take up too much time.
- Plan carefully. Don't let expenses slyly gobble up profits.
- Money earned in the name of Camp Fire Girls is used for Camp Fire purposes only. Earnings are never used for a girl's personal use outside of Camp Fire.

Councilwide Sale

Most groups take part in an annual councilwide sale which is arranged by the Camp Fire Girls council. This is a fine way to Give Service to your council and your national organization. It tells many people about Camp Fire Girls. It helps you learn how to be businesslike, how to make change, how to keep records, how to meet people. It helps your group earn the major part of your necessary group expenses, for national membership dues, Camp Fire books, some honor beads, fun and service projects. You'll earn Camp Fire honors too. Don't plan other money-earning when it's councilwide sale time. Also follow the "Safety Guides for Sales" in Chapter 20.

More Ways to Earn Money

- A Flower Cart Sale of home grown flowers or plants
- A Made-It-Myself Food Sale. Be sure it's good!
- Seven Crafts Fair. Be proud to say "Made by Camp Fire Girls."
- A Play or Puppet Show. What fun to make scenery and stage!
- An Outdoor Carnival or Back Yard Circus for neighborhood children
- An International Doll Show with a small fee for each entry.

You'll have other ideas. Just be sure it's something you'll be proud of and that will help you learn new things and have fun.

Making a Group Budget

A budget is a plan to help your group pay its own way. It shows you:

1. how much money your group needs for such things as
   - a copy of the BOOK OF THE CAMP FIRE GIRLS for each member
   - national membership dues for each girl
   - honor beads (usually the group pays for a certain number per member)
   - group projects
   - group supplies and equipment
2. how much you plan to receive in group dues
3. how much you need to earn, to do the things you want to do

The following Sample Budget Form shows you one way to make a budget. This should give you an idea of how you want to do yours. Begin with a large sheet of paper which everyone can see and comment on. Try making your own!

A SAMPLE BUDGET FORM

INCOME

WEEKLY DUES

_____ girls @ _____ ¢ = $_____ , x weeks   = $_____

MONEY WE'LL EARN

a. Annual councilwide sale   _____
b. Our group play   _____
c. Food sale   _____

Total income $_____

EXPENSES

NATIONAL MEMBERSHIP DUES

_____ girls @ $2.00   = $_____

GROUP SUPPLIES OR ACTIVITIES

a. _____ books @ $1.00   _____
b. 15 Honor Beads per member   _____
c. _____   _____

Total expenses $_____

IF TOTAL INCOME EQUALS TOTAL EXPENSES, THE BUDGET BALANCES.

Your Money and You

Making Your Own Budget

Not only your group has exciting plans. Probably _you_ have some big plans, too. Some will be with your group, some with your family, and some just your own. Usually, these cost money.

If you receive an allowance, this pays for part of your expenses. Probably you earn money for the rest. But are you making the most of your money? Are you using it to go where it means the most to you? This isn't easy for girls to make happen. It isn't easy for adults, either.

Keeping track of your money does help you learn to stretch your budget. That means noticing how you get it and how you spend it. By knowing this, you may be able to make your money go further.

Do you find you need more money? All right, put on your thinking cap. See how you can earn more money. Or, are you "wasting" money on things you could do without? Is there something you'd rather have? Start planning.

You can keep track of your money by becoming a *thriftee*. This is a requirement for the rank of Fire Maker, so you will want to do it then. Some girls try it before then, too.

Becoming a Thriftee

Whether you have five cents or five dollars, write down every bit of money you receive, spend, and save. If you have an allowance, write it down when you receive it. If you receive money to purchase clothes, lunches, books, or to pay dues or to contribute to your church or synagogue, write it down. Do this regularly for four weeks. You can start any time, but it's easier to start on the first of the month.

Here is an easy way to make your own Thriftee Book. Use a simple notebook. Rule the pages something like this:

My Thriftee Book

Month	Day	Received	Spent	Saved	Remarks
May	1	X.xx			my allowance
		X.xx			earned
				.xx	for camp
	3		.xx		group dues
	4		.xx		gave in church
	5	X.xx			birthday present!
			X.xx		school lunches, May 1-5
Total:		**X.xx**	**X.xx**	**.xx**	

Balance on hand: X.xx ("Spent" and "saved," subtracted from "received")

This example shows only five days. Yours would continue. When you come to the bottom of a page, total the columns and show the balance. This balance is carried forward to the next page.

Part 2

GROWING IN CAMP FIRE

YOUR THREE CAMP FIRE RANKS

The good times you have, the skills you learn and share, and the progress you will make on the Camp Fire trail are marked by three Camp Fire ranks: Trail Seeker, Wood Gatherer, and Fire Maker.

Where do you start?
As we mentioned before,

— if you're nine years old or in the fourth grade, you're ready to start toward Trail Seeker.

— if you are ten or in the fifth grade, you may start toward becoming a Wood Gatherer.

— if you're eleven or in the sixth grade, you may start to become a Fire Maker.

(When you're a Junior Hi Camp Fire Girl you may become a Torch Bearer, but that's when you're older . . . about twelve or thirteen.)

• Becoming a Trail Seeker means you seek or look for a good path to follow in life. In trying out this path, there will be hikes with lunches eaten out of doors, service given to others, Indian symbol games and your first group ceremonial. You'll help to plan a party and a trip and do many other things in this rank.

• Becoming a Wood Gatherer means that by following your path with others in your group, you try to become a better person: to progress, to learn, to accomplish, to share with your group. You'll enjoy games and dances, an exciting symbol project, making friends with people from other countries while learning to be a good citizen of your own country. There will be cookouts, dramatics, ceremonials, and you'll decorate your ceremonial costume.

• Becoming a Fire Maker means you are becoming a better person and a nearly grown-up one: taking responsibility, giving service, sharing with others your skills and your joys on the Camp Fire trail. Sports and games parties, cookouts and camping trips help you keep fit in body and mind. Learning to be a gracious hostess will help to prepare you for growing up and liking it. Here you'll have a real service project of your own choosing, and a new creative arts experience for you and your group.

Desires for Ranks

Each rank has its own Desire which will mean something personal to you as you work toward and complete each rank. These Desires help you learn a beautiful way of saying what you want to be and the kind of girl you want to become.

Insignia of Ranks

Each rank has its own insigne or symbol with its special meaning.

Trail Seeker's Charm

The symbols for *flame* and *path* on the Trail Seeker's silver finish charm mean the beginning of adventures for you on the Camp Fire trail.

Wood Gatherer's Ring

The *fagot* (bundle of sticks) on the silver finish Wood Gatherer's ring represents your Camp Fire group bound together in friendship and loyalty. The three *dots* symbolize Work, Health and Love.

Fire Maker's Bracelet

On the Fire Maker's bracelet is our watchword, Wohelo, written in Alaskan Indian letters. This silver finish band is a symbol of what you have done to enrich your life and the lives of those around you.

After you have earned the right to wear these, you can wear them every day if you wish, not just with your ceremonial costume.

Ranks and the Seven Crafts

One requirement in each rank is that girls *earn honors* (do activities) in each of the Seven Crafts. Girls often find that as they do other requirements for rank, they are earning additional honors. Each honor activity means that you have grown a little more.

For each honor activity you do, you are entitled to wear a small wooden honor bead. This is a symbol of what you have done to earn that honor. The colors and the shapes of the honor beads are different for each of the Seven Crafts, and these colors have special meaning. You can find out more about this by looking in Chapter 8.

When You Finish a Rank

You will work toward one rank at a time. When you have completed your work for a rank, you will need to have a conference with your guardian and sponsors. Tell or show them your record of honors and activities in this rank. You and they will want to be sure you have done your best when you achieve a rank in Camp Fire.

Recognition for Rank

When you have completed a rank, your group — sometimes with other groups—will have a beautiful ceremonial. Each girl who has completed a rank receives:

1. A Certificate of Rank, for the rank she has earned
2. Purple achievement beads. Purple stands for *achievement*

   5 beads for the rank of Trail Seeker
   10 beads for the rank of Wood Gatherer
   15 beads for the rank of Fire Maker

   These are small beads. The large purple bead may *not* be substituted, being earned for the rank of Torch Bearer.
3. Honor beads in the Seven Crafts which she has earned while working on this rank, (if she has not already received these)

You are then entitled to wear the insigne of each rank, as mentioned before.

TRAIL SEEKER'S DESIRE

I desire
To seek the way
That shall become
A delight to my feet,
For it will bring me
To the fire of human kindness
Lighted by those
Who have gone before me
On the Camp Fire trail.

THEODORE A. HARPER

SYMBOLS IN THE ▱ thought = desire to seek the . . . . .
BACKGROUND ▲ heart = fire of human kindness
DESIGN ARE ⁞⁞⁞⁞⁞⁞ path = on the camp fire trail

REQUIREMENTS FOR TRAIL SEEKER RANK

Becoming a Trail Seeker is your first step on the Camp Fire trail if you are nine years old or in the fourth grade. You must be an active *registered member of your group for at least four months* to become a Trail Seeker. These are the things you *will* do to achieve this rank.

Note: The double box beside each requirement is to help you keep your record, like this:

Date Completed 4/10/6-	Guardian's initials G. H. H.

Getting Acquainted With Camp Fire

1. Name the 3 ranks in Camp Fire and the Seven Crafts. Describe the color symbolism of the 7 different honor beads. Tell the meaning of the watchword and the slogan.

2. Make plans with your group and go on a hike. Take a trailside lunch which you prepared yourself. Look and listen for interesting things in nature. Tell your group about 2 or 3.

3. Learn the Trail Seeker's Desire. Talk with your guardian about what it means to you. Describe the symbols on the Trail Seeker's charm.

4. Complete at least 2 honors in each of the Seven Crafts. Keep a record of the honors you earn.

Service—Symbols—Ceremonials

5. Give Service to others by doing 1 of the following, and if possible, delivering it in person:

   a. Make decorations for a hospital, children's home or day nursery.

   b. Make a gift for an elderly person or a shut-in child.

   c. Gather material and make dish gardens or seasonal bouquets for shut-ins.

6. With your group, find out about American Indian symbols and how the Indians use them. Do 1 of the following:

   a. Play 2 or 3 symbol games, using at least 6 different Indian symbols.

   b. Help to make or draw a group picture story, using 6 or more Indian symbols.

   c. Use 6 Indian symbols in making something, like invitations or decorations.

7. Take part in your group ceremonial meetings. Receive the honor beads you have earned. Sing songs you have learned in your group, choosing some from this book.

Telling the Story—Choosing My Name—A Trip

8. Help your group to make plans for a meeting for your parents, sponsors, or teachers. Tell them about Camp Fire Girls and when and where the organization started; do this by acting, talking, or drawing. Have games, songs, and refreshments.

9. Choose a Camp Fire name for yourself. Before choosing your name, tell your guardian what you want it to mean to you.

10. Make plans with your group and visit an interesting place like a science or nature or art museum or a zoo, where you will see and learn something new. Match memories and talk about your new experiences in a group meeting after the trip.

Hints for Doing The Trail Seeker's Rank

Doesn't it seem that an exciting year is in store for you and your group working toward becoming a Trail Seeker? All the basic information you need to learn to complete this rank is right here in this book. Get acquainted with the table of contents and the index, and they will help you find what you are interested in.

Just to be sure you are started in the right way, here are some hints for doing the Trail Seeker's Rank.

TS #1. To find the names of the three ranks, look back to the contents page. Find a chapter called "Your Three Camp Fire Ranks." On what page does it start? Surprise—you are in that chapter now! Of course you already know one rank, because this is the rank you are interested in doing. Now keep looking through this chapter, and you will find the other two. Easy? Sure it is.

The part about the Seven Crafts you can look up in just the same way. The chapter by that name also tells you about the color symbolism of the seven different honor beads. (The information about rank achievement beads is in *this* chapter.)

Another part of this requirement is telling the meaning of our watchword and slogan. In checking to see what these meanings are, let's go back to the contents page. Do you find them there? No. That means that there isn't an entire chapter about the watchword and the slogan. Next stop? You guessed right if you thought of the index at the back of the book. Look for both words. On what page are they found? Now check to see if the information you need is really there. It is, isn't it?

From here on, try checking this information yourself. All the information you need to get started on the projects described will be there. First look in the table of contents, and if what you are looking for isn't there, go to the index. It *always* should be there!

Seven Crafts Guessing Game: On slips of paper write the names of the three ranks, and the names and colors of the Seven Crafts. Cut apart the names of the ranks, and cut the Crafts apart from the colors. Example: "Trail" and "Seeker" would be partners. "Citizenship" and "Red, white, and blue" would be partners. Mix them and have each girl draw *one* slip of paper. Match partners by matching names and colors.

Each pair then acts out name of the rank or Craft, saying, "This is a rank" or "This is one of the Seven Crafts." The other girls try to guess which one.

TS #2. Where do you hike? Outdoors, of course. Look under the heading, *Outdoors,* for ideas for your trailside lunch and hike.

TS #3. Finding the Trail Seeker's Desire is not hard, is it? But telling what it means in your own words may be a little more so.

"I desire to seek the way that shall become a delight to my feet. . . ." To "desire" is to want to do something. To "seek the way" is to want to find out *how to do* things.

What does "a delight to my feet" mean? Soft green grass, moss, cool sand or water? Perhaps, but to you as a Trail Seeker it means something else. It means that you've found *pleasure* and *joy* and *beauty* in Camp Fire Girls.

". . . For it will bring me to the fire of human kindness . . ." This means that by finding kind things to do for others, by being a thoughtful girl, you will find many friends. You'll have a warm feeling in your heart when you think of the smile in your guardian's eyes, and the friendship circle in your group.

". . . Lighted by those who have gone before me on the Camp Fire trail." Just think! Since Dr. and Mrs. Luther H. Gulick, our founders, started Camp Fire Girls in 1910, thousands of guardians and girls and others have helped to make Camp Fire come true for you, and girls everywhere today.

TS #4. You'll have a good time doing this!

TS #5. One way to Give Service is to help your group make a "Happy-talk Box." Small things, wrapped in gay papers, would be fun for someone who is ill or shut in.

Things for a "Happy-talk Box"

A little gift you've made	A pencil and pad of paper
A picture story or cartoon	Tiny garden in a shell or paper cup
Tray or bedside table favors	Decoration for holiday or birthday
Greeting card from your group	What else can you think of?

If your box is for a hospital or children's home or day nursery, it could be chock full of holiday or birthday decorations. What would *you* like to find in it? Paper hats, fancy napkins, favors for a tray or for a centerpiece? If you cannot deliver it in person, enclose a note to the children, saying they are going to have a party *with* you, even though you are not together.

Give Service Quiz: Divide the group into two or more teams. See how many ways each team can think of for girls to give service during the coming week, or on a special day like a holiday or a Sunday. Have a time limit. When time is up each team acts out one idea for giving service. The others try to guess. After each team has performed, list *all* the ideas each team thought of, and see how many different ways you've discovered to Give Service.

TS #6. In order to do this requirement, you'll want to look through still another chapter in this book. Your guardian will help you and your group explore many interesting games and projects to learn about American Indian symbolism.

TS #7. One more chapter will help your group get started on having ceremonials. (You'll like them, and this is the only way girls can receive their honor beads and recognition for rank.)

TS #8. Your group will have many ideas for fulfilling this requirement. This is a grand way to say "Hello," "Thank You," or "We Love You." Remember to:

1. start your plans several weeks in advance.

2. make and send invitations.

3. decide what kind of "entertainment" you'll have. Will you sing some songs, and tell something about Camp Fire Girls: how they began, and what you are like or do now? This probably will take some special practice.

4. plan refreshments. Most groups think that baking cookies, making the tea or punch, or preparing whichever simple refreshments are chosen is a big part of the fun.

TS #9. A name you chose for yourself is your Camp Fire name. The index lists the page which will guide you in going about this.

TS #10. Talk over with your group where you would like to go, and try to find a place your group has not been before. There is always something exciting for Camp Fire Girls to discover and explore.

At your next meeting, take turns telling about what you discovered on the trip, either along the way or at the museum or whatever place your group visited.

WOOD GATHERER'S DESIRE

As fagots are brought
   from the forest
Firmly held by the sinews
   which bind them,
I will cleave to my
   Camp Fire sisters
Wherever, whenever
   I find them.
I will strive to grow
   strong like the pine tree;
To be pure in my
   deepest desire;
To be true to the truth
   that is in me,
And follow the
   Law of Camp Fire.

SYMBOLS IN THE 〓 fagots = kinship in our Camp Fire group
BACKGROUND ▲ hand = strive to grow and continue to
DESIGN ARE ‖‖‖‖path = follow the Camp Fire trail

REQUIREMENTS FOR WOOD GATHERER RANK

Becoming a Wood Gatherer is the second step on the Camp Fire trail to fun and friendship. Most of the requirements are things which your group would probably decide to do anyway, but they will also help you along the path toward growing up and being a better person.

You may begin working toward this rank if you are a Trail Seeker, *or* if you are ten years old, *or* in the fifth grade. Every girl needs to know certain things about Camp Fire Girls. If you are a *new* member, do these things right away:

a. Learn the watchword, slogan, and the meaning and value of achieving the three ranks.

b. Learn the colors, the meaning, and the value of earning the honor beads in the Seven Crafts.

c. Choose your Camp Fire name and tell its meaning.

You must be a *registered member and active in your group for at least four months,* as you do the following things to become a Wood Gatherer.

Note: The double box opposite each requirement is to help you keep your record, like this:

Date completed 11/6/6-	Guardian's Initials G. H. H.

Learning—Helping to Enjoy—Exploring

1. Learn the Wood Gatherer's Desire and in your own words explain its meaning. Describe the symbolism of the Wood Gatherer's ring.

2. Help your group enjoy sports and games by doing 1 of the following:

   a. Take an active part in 2 outdoor or indoor sports or games or folk dances. Help to lead or teach 1 of them.

   b. With another group, learn and dance 2 or 3 square or country dances. Do them several times in your group.

3. Complete 2 or more honors, new to you in *each* Craft. Record your honors.

Symbols—Citizenship—Hikes

4. Discover how symbols are used by many people and for many purposes 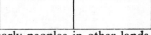 by the American Indians, by early peoples in other lands, and today in business, music, art, religion, travel. Do 1 of the following with your group:

   a. Have Symbol Day. See how many symbols you can observe all day, indoors and out. Collect pictures, drawings or cutouts of symbols. Make a group symbol scrapbook or a symbol exhibit to share your discoveries with others.

   b. Plan and go on a symbol hike. See how many different symbols, hand signs and symbol sounds you can observe in use around your town or neighborhood.

5. Discuss why and demonstrate how we show honor and respect to the 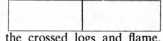 flag of the United States of America. Demonstrate how to fold the flag, how to display and use it.

6. Tell why the name Camp Fire Girls was chosen for our organization. 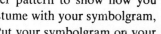 Explain the symbolism of the crossed logs and flame, insigne of Camp Fire Girls.

7. Make your own Camp Fire symbolgram in color and explain what 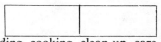 it means to you. Then make a paper pattern to show how you plan to decorate your ceremonial costume with your symbolgram, honor beads and insignia of ranks. Put your symbolgram on your ceremonial costume or headband.

8. Help plan and go on an all-day hike or trip and have a cookout with your group. Help with fire building, cooking, clean-up, care of camp site, and safety precautions.

Ceremonials—Service—International Friendship

9. Help to plan and take part in at least 2 group ceremonials, wearing your Camp Fire costume. Invite your parents to one of these. Sing 4 or 5 songs chosen from Camp Fire Girls books.

10. Give Service in 1 of the following
    ways:

    a. Tell others about Camp Fire Girls by taking part in a program
       such as a demonstration or exhibit of the Seven Crafts, a radio
       broadcast or a television show, a presentation of Camp Fire
       songs or ceremonies.

    b. Give a show about the Camp Fire Girls. It could be a shadow
       play or other dramatic presentation, a scroll show, or a choral
       speaking activity. Make the puppets and scenery when neces-
       sary. Present the show to others: shut-ins, younger children,
       older people, or another Camp Fire group.

11. Make a friend and be one. Help
    your group to do 1 of these:

    a. Have an International Friendship Party. Find out about and
       plan food, music and decorations to show understanding and
       appreciation of people in other countries.

    b. Have an International Friendship Tea. Invite a guest to tell
       the group about another country and its children, costumes,
       crafts, and schools. Have refreshments and table decorations
       typical of that country.

Note: Whether this is your first or second Camp Fire rank, becoming
a Wood Gatherer is a big step forward. Consult your good
friends, the table of contents and the index, for the information
you need to complete this rank.

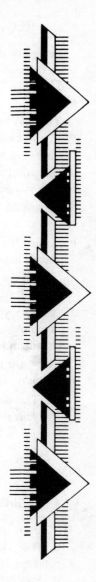

FIRE MAKER'S DESIRE

As fuel is brought to the fire
So I purpose to bring
My strength
My ambition
My heart's desire
My joy
And my sorrow
To the fire
Of humankind;
For I will tend
As my fathers have tended
And my fathers' fathers
Since time began
The fire that is called
The love of man for man,
The love of man for God.

JOHN COLLIER

SYMBOLS IN THE ≋ fagots = fuel ... star ┽┾ = purpose .. ambition
BACKGROUND △ heart = desire .. thoughts ∥ = joy and sorrow
DESIGN ARE ⟊ hand = to bring path ⁑⁑⁑ = camp fire trail

REQUIREMENTS FOR FIRE MAKER RANK

Becoming a Fire Maker is the third step along the Camp Fire trail toward becoming a better person, taking responsibility, giving service, and sharing with others your skills and your joys on the Camp Fire trail.

You may begin working toward this rank if you are a Wood Gatherer, *or* if you're eleven years old, *or* in the sixth grade.

There are basic things every Camp Fire Girl needs to know about her organization and its unique features. Be sure you do these things right away *if you are a new member:*

a. Learn the watchword, slogan, and the meaning and value of achieving Camp Fire ranks.

b. Learn the color symbolism, meaning, and value of earning honor beads in the Seven Crafts.

c. Learn the meaning of the name and insigne of the Camp Fire Girls organization.

d. Choose your Camp Fire name and tell its meaning. Make your symbolgram in color and put it on your ceremonial costume or headband.

You must be *a registered member, active in your group for at least six months,* and do the following while becoming a Fire Maker.

Note: The double box beside each requirement is for you to keep your record like this:

Date Completed 5/4/6-	Guardian's Initials G. H. H.

A Girl's Goals—Sports and Games—New Adventures

1. Learn the Fire Maker's Desire. Write, illustrate, or tell what it means to you; share this with your guardian and your parents. Describe the symbolism of the Fire Maker's bracelet.

2. Take part in giving a party whose theme is based on the Sports and Games Craft, for guests of your own age. Help to plan invitations, hostess duties, refreshments, and program.

3. Be an active and responsible member of a committee. Help to plan, carry out and evaluate group activity, such as those in #2, 5, 10.

4. Discover new adventures in the Seven Crafts. Earn and record 20 honors which you have not earned before, at least 2 in *each* Craft, and 3 additional ones in your *two favorite* Crafts.

Tell your group about 1 honor activity which gave you a new experience or helped you to learn a new skill or to form a good habit.

Camping Trips—"Thriftees"—Joy of Service

5. Camping is fun! Help to plan and go on 1 of the following camping trips with your group:

   a. An overnight trip with 3 of the meals cooked outdoors.

   b. Two 1-day trips (not consecutive), cooking 1 meal outdoors each day.

   Share responsibility in planning menus, purchasing food, planning program, and packing equipment. In a group meeting after the trip, discuss your experiences and make notes on how to improve plans for the next trip.

6. Be a "Thriftee"! Keep a record of all money you receive, spend and save, for 4 weeks.

7. With your group, find out what you can do to Give Service to your community, country, or overseas. Choose and carry out a service project alone or with your group.

Ceremonials—Gracious Living—Lively Arts—Looking Ahead

8. Take part in at least 2 group ceremonials; use symbolism. Help to plan 1 of them. Do 1 of the following:

   a. Write a candle or fire lighting ceremony to be used by your group.

    b. With your group, visit a new group or invite them to share in a ceremonial to learn about Camp Fire Girls.

    c. Invite a guest. Help to tell or illustrate the program of Camp Fire Girls from Blue Birds through Horizon Club.

9. Be a gracious hostess. With a committee of not more than 5 other girls, prepare and serve indoors or in a patio or porch, 1 luncheon or dinner. This includes planning the menu, purchasing the food, cooking and serving a balanced meal attractively, acting as a hostess, and cleaning up. Evaluate the project with the committee and your guardian afterwards.

10. Help to plan and carry out 1 group project, having to do with drama, music, art, literature, or science, such as:

    a. Write an original story and present it in dramatic form for an audience. The presentation should include scenery, costumes, and background music. — OR —

    Put this story in book, record, or tape recording form, including appropriate illustrations or sound effects. Give this to some one who would appreciate it: a school or public library, the children's ward of the hospital, a shut-in, or other.

    b. Make up a song or other piece of music. Write it out on music staff paper. Include an accompaniment if it is appropriate. Teach the song to another group.

    c. Sponsor a Creative Arts show in which every member of your group will be proud to display something she has created: sculpture, music, a painting, a mobile, poetry, a story, etc. Others may be invited to exhibit, too.

    d. Have a Science Craft exhibit, where simple experiments can be demonstrated by members of your group, and scientific hobbies can be displayed. Invite another group, or parents, to the exhibit, or present it for a club or an adult group.

11. As a group, look to the future to learn what awaits you in Junior Hi Camp Fire Girls. Do 1 of these:

    a. Invite a Junior Hi Camp Fire group to a party, so that they can tell you what lies ahead for you in Junior Hi Camp Fire Girls.

b. Look through the *Book of the Junior Hi Camp Fire Girls,* especially at the Group Torch Bearer rank. Discuss this together, and share your opinions on why Junior Hi Camp Fire Girls is for you.

c. Invite some one who belonged to Camp Fire Girls as a teenager, to tell you what she remembers about growing up in Camp Fire Girls during her junior high years.

Note: Information and suggestions for ways to do these requirements are found in this book. The table of contents and index will direct you.

HONORS IN THE SEVEN CRAFTS

HONORS FINDER

HONORS IN THE SEVEN CRAFTS

The Seven Crafts open seven doors for you. Look inside, and you will find many adventures to explore, for among them they represent the seven main interests of most girls. Do you agree? In alphabet order, they are: Business Craft, Citizenship Craft, Creative Arts Craft, Home Craft, Outdoors Craft, Science Craft, and Sports and Games Craft.

Honors

The Seven Crafts are made up of honors. What are those? Honors are girl-sized do-it-yourself activities. They are something new and interesting learned, a good habit formed, or a service given. Some are easy; others are really hard—but fun! Some you can do just by yourself; some you may do with other girls. There are many of both kinds you will want to choose and try right away. See for yourself.

Honor Beads

When you have completed an honor in a Craft, you have earned the right to wear an honor bead. This becomes a symbol of your accomplishment. For a Business Craft honor, you earn a yellow honor bead. For a Sports and Games Craft honor, you earn a red honor bead. Each of the Seven Crafts has its special honor bead with its own shape, color, and meaning.

Try coloring the honor beads shown here the proper color, to help you learn which honor bead stands for each Craft.

1. Business Craft honor beads are yellow. They are a symbol of the harvest, of work done happily with good results.

2. Citizenship Craft honor beads are red, white, and blue, the colors of the flag of the United States of America where Camp Fire Girls was founded. These colors stand for good citizenship in our homes, at school, church or synagogue, in our community, and the world.

3. Creative Arts Craft honor beads are green, nature's color

of creation and growing things. Dramatics, dancing, music, hand arts, writing, and other ways of creating beauty are in this Craft.

4. Home Craft honor beads are flame color. Flame is symbolic of the hearth fire of the home. In this Craft is the service girls give to their homes and to their families.

5. Outdoors Craft honor beads are brown; that reminds us of earth, tree trunks, the woods, and wildlife. Hiking, camping, exploring, and nature hobbies are found in this Craft.

6. Science Craft honor beads are blue. They symbolize the sky, which extends to ever-widening horizons of scientific knowledge. In this Craft there are experiments with sound, heat, plants, and other interests.

7. Sports and Games Craft honor beads are red for your apple-red cheeks, for good health, and keeping physically fit. Games and exercise, outdoors and in, active skills, and good sportsmanship are in this Craft.

The honor beads which you earn are a way of showing your personal growth in Camp Fire Girls. Each tells its own story of learning, stretching, sharing, or work well done. They are worn proudly on or with your ceremonial costume because they symbolize activities done successfully. Every girl decides how she wishes to arrange her beads, in attractive designs. Because they are an *honor* to wear, they are so named: *honor beads*.

As you grow in Camp Fire you will have many honor beads. You may choose to wear one large honor bead with, or in place of, ten small ones in any one Craft. Let's say you have earned ten Science Craft honors, and you received ten small blue honor beads. You may also wear one *large* Science Craft honor bead, either *with* or *instead of* the ten small ones. (*NOTE:* This is true only of the Seven Crafts honor beads. It is *not* true of the purple beads which you receive when you achieve rank.)

When Have You Earned An Honor?

Many girls have questions about, "When have I earned an honor?" The first thing you will need to know is what this mark * means, when it follows an honor. An honor with * means you can *repeat* the honor

5 or 6 times, by doing the *same* thing. These are good habit-forming activities. Honors without the * you can earn more than once by doing the activity a *different* way. That means you *do* something new and *learn* something new.

The second thing you must do, to know when you have earned an honor, is to ask yourself these questions. Each answer should be yes.

1. Are you a registered member of Camp Fire Girls? Have you paid your dues to Camp Fire Girls, Inc.?

2. Did you complete the honor to the best of your ability?

3. Did you learn something new, give service, or begin to form a good habit?

"How many honor beads can I get?" is not important; "How much did I learn, or help, or try?" is very important.

If you have answered yes to all the above questions, talk about it with an adult—a parent, your guardian, or another adult friend. This is the final way to help you decide when you have earned an honor.

When the two of you have agreed that you have earned the honor, ask this person to initial and date your record of this. Or, take a signed statement from this person to your guardian, so that she can initial and date your honors record.

Keeping A Record of Honors and Ranks Earned

Just how you keep a record of the honors you earn and the ranks you achieve is up to you, but you must be sure to keep it carefully. A well-kept record is important so that you can see what progress you are making in Camp Fire. This is important to your guardian, too, for she checks *her* records of your progress against yours. Every time your group plans a ceremonial, her records tell her how many honor beads to order for you.

There are pages at the end of this book where you may record your honors, or you may prefer to list them in an honors and ranks book which you make. Some girls may choose to make a larger Camp Fire book and include their symbolgram, snapshots, and souvenirs of group experiences, as well as a record of the ranks and honors achieved.

A Sample Record of Honors Achieved

RECORD OF MY HONOR ACHIEVEMENTS

*The adult is your mother, guardian, teacher, camp counselor or other adult who knows you earned this honor.

Craft and Honor Number	What I Did to Earn an Honor (For fun draw a pictograph of the honor) ▶	*Initials of Adult	Date Beads Received
Home 413	Planned table decorations and favors for Dad's birthday party.	EMK	6/10/6-
Bus. 143	I brought a new member to our group.		
Science 1001	I wrote a letter with invisible ink.		
	Etc.		

Here Are the Honors!

It's a wise Camp Fire Girl who plans ahead, choosing which honors she wishes to earn before the rush of her first ceremonial—or the next and the next. How do you begin? It's easy! Look at the headings at the begining of each Craft. That will give you a good idea about what each Craft has in store for you. Now look at the honors under some of these headings. Do you find some you'd like to do right away? If you do, that's fine. Choose any you wish.

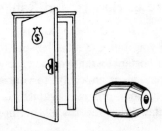

Business Craft

Developing Businesslike Habits

101 Save money you have earned or money you receive from your allowance, to buy something you need.

102 Save money you have earned or money you receive from your

allowance, to buy a gift for someone else.

103 Be on time for school, Camp Fire meetings, lessons, and all appointments, for at least 2 months.*

104 Do not borrow articles for 2 consecutive months.*

105 Keep your shoes polished and in good repair for at least 1 month.*

106 Take good care of your skates for at least 2 months. Keep them clean, in repair, and store them in a safe place.

107 Take good care of your bicycle for at least 2 months; keep it clean, in repair, and parked in its proper place.

108 Wash the windows of the family automobile, inside and out, once a week for 1 month.

109 Wash and clean an automobile.

110 Clean and wax an automobile.

111 Make a collection of recipes for economical meals. Select 2; visit a market and make a list of the actual costs of foods needed for these.

112 Visit a construction job in your town (house, office building, etc.) with your family or friends. Observe the materials used; find out why these are used and why they are suitable for the type of building.

113 Cut advertisements from daily newspapers to show the cost of furnishing different rooms in a house. Give a brief talk on the cost of furnishing 1 room.

114 Interview 1 of the following: The postman, policeman, librarian, doctor, or any other interesting adult. Report to your group on what this person does and some interesting things about his job.

115 Make a simple street map of your community or neighborhood, showing where stores, factories, schools, and churches are located. List the kinds of businesses and institutions in this area.

116 Make a listing of good radio and television programs for children. Include name of program, station, time. Share it with your group.

117 Prepare a program illustrating businesslike appearance and conduct. Do this with your group. Include dress, hair and nails, posture.

118 Find out how to get 1 of the following: a) A copy of your birth certificate. b) A photostatic copy of a valuable paper or manuscript. c) A copyright for a song or publication. d) A patent.

119 Write, on the proper forms, a night letter, a day letter, and a telegram. Find out the number of words allowed in each, difference in cost and delivery time, and how to send and pay for such a message by telephone or from the telegraph office.

120 Write or visit a pet store and learn what is needed to keep certain kinds of pets, the costs for food, and special equipment needed.

121 Learn requirements for owning and keeping a dog, such as where to get a dog license, how to arrange for inoculations for pets, and other such needs.

122 Take care of a canary or other pet bird for 2 months. Include feeding and care of cage. Pay for food and supplies from your allowance or personal budget.*

123 Purchase fish with money you have earned, and stock an aquarium or fish bowl. Take care of it for 2 months.*

124 Feed and care for a pet animal for 1 month.*

125 Make application and exhibit your pet (bird, cat, dog, etc.) in a local pet show. Groom it for the show, take it and stay with it during the show.*

126 Discuss with adults their ideas on giving tips. With your group, set up a scale for tipping for services rendered, which will be suitable in your area.

127 Show a younger person how to use a telephone directory, dial a number, and answer a telephone properly.

128 Show a younger person how to use a dictionary, encyclopedia, or atlas.

129 Conduct a guided tour for a new girl in your school or neighborhood. Point out places of interest to her and her family, such as the local bank, telephone company, department stores.

130 Discover the time zones in the United States: (Pacific zone, Mountain zone, etc.) Explain how many zones there are, why the time changes, and where the International Date Line is.

131 Escort your mother or father or another adult to a Camp Fire meeting planned for them.

132 Demonstrate at a Camp Fire meeting the proper way to introduce a speaker to your group, and the proper way to introduce your mother to your guardian.

133 At a Camp Fire meeting write an invitation to a party or a tea, and a thank-you note for help given to your group by a sponsor.

134 Index neatly your *Book of the Camp Fire Girls* with tabs marking each important section of your book.

135 Take care of all group equipment for 1 month, taking care to see that all items are returned and properly stored.*

136 Serve as a telephone committee-of-one. Call girls and remind them about a special event: time, place, what to wear, money needed, special jobs.

137 Write a letter to a business or factory asking if your group may visit it.

138 Submit articles telling of your group events to your council newsletter (or local newspaper), for 2 months.

139 Serve as treasurer of your group for at least 2 months, keeping accounts and having them checked by your guardian.

140 Serve as secretary of your Camp Fire group for at least 2 months, keeping proper records of meetings.

141 Serve as president of your group for at least 2 months, conducting meetings in accordance with simplified parliamentary law.

142 Serve as the chairman of an active committee for your group or class.*

143 Secure and get registered 1 new member for your group, or for a group in any other program level in Camp Fire Girls.*

144 Prepare a roster of the names, addresses, and telephone numbers of each member of your group. Give a copy to each member.

145 Help plan, and go with your group, to a restaurant for dinner. Before you go, discuss how to read a menu, order a meal, and how to tip.

146 Help your group discuss and make up a set of safety rules to follow when you participate in the Camp Fire Girls community-wide sale.

147 Act out how to approach prospective customers when you are selling something to earn money for Camp Fire Girls. Practice how to tell the customer about Camp Fire Girls, and how to be gracious whether or not you make a sale.

Earning Money

201 Pay your Camp Fire national annual membership dues from money you have earned or saved.*

202 Earn 1 dollar and give it to a charity, church or community interest.*

203 Earn enough money to buy at least 1 dollar's worth of school supplies.

204 Sell produce (vegetables, fruit, flowers, berries, eggs, etc.) at your family's wayside market or vegetable and fruit stand. Keep an account of your sales.

205 Sell 6 tickets for a Camp Fire puppet show, play, carnival, art show, etc.

206 Serve as cashier at a sale or event. Balance the account and give the money to the proper person.

207 Help your group plan and carry out a money raising project.

208 Take an active part in a sale, bazaar, or other money earning project for Camp Fire Girls, in which 3 or more groups participate. Always go with another girl when you sell or deliver.*

Shopping and Purchasing

301 Talk over with adults in your family 10 brand products recommended in TV commericals; discuss why or why not each is used in your home.

302 Talk over with a parent some major purchase that is being considered by the family. Find out if, why, when, where, it may be purchased, and how the choice is made between brands. If possible, go along when it is purchased.

303 Assist your mother when she plans the food marketing for the family for 1 week. Go to the store with her and keep a list of what she buys and the cost.

304 The following week, plan what food will need to be purchased for the family. Make a shopping list and have your mother check it. Go to the store and buy the food on your list.

305 Help an adult with the weekly grocery shopping for 4 weeks. Find out what her reasons are for buying certain brands, certain sizes of cans and packages, etc.

306 Check prices, after at least 4 shopping trips, by comparing the cash register slip with the prices marked on articles and the number of articles bought.

307 Purchase the food for an entire family dinner. Keep an account of the cost. Do this with the advice of an adult.

308 Compare prices of 3 brands, of each of 3 different food products. Explain what accounts for the price difference.

309 Visit a supermarket and compare the prices, of 4 vegetables or

fruits, the fresh and the frozen form. Explain what accounts for the difference in cost.

310 Help plan and shop for a party or special celebration given in your home. Include planning of costs.*

311 Help the group to plan and shop for the food that will be needed for a group cookout. Include planning of cost.*

312 Have the responsibility for purchasing Camp Fire materials for a special project or activity, for your group. Keep a careful account of expenditures.*

313 Serve as an active member of the purchasing committee for an event to which others are invited. Request receipt and account for purchases. Make a financial report to the group.

314 Compare the differences in price and quality of several items of girls' clothing such as socks, shoes, skirts, blouses. Do this by checking local newspaper advertisements, and by visiting a clothing store.

315 Make a list with the assistance of an adult of all the clothes you need for the coming season. Make an estimate of the total cost.*

316 Assist in the purchase of 6 different kinds of items from the above list. For each kind of item, compare styles and prices in the store and read all tags.*

317 Plan your shoe purchases for the coming season: types for different occasions, suitability of different materials, total cost. Talk over with an adult, and help in buying.*

318 Make a list for each member of your family, of sizes and preferences (color, etc.). Include what will be helpful to you when you select a gift for any of them.

319 Compare bus and train fares for a trip your group plans to take. Report this and any reservations requirements to the others.

320 Compare the costs of the different classes of air travel to a place you would like to visit. Learn how you would make a reservation.

Budgets and Records

401 Keep a daily diary for 1 month.*

402 Keep a personal detailed record of every cent you receive, spend, and save for 1 month.*

403 Make yourself a time schedule, and try to keep it. Include time for the different things you do: at school, at home, and in your community.

404 Keep a record for 2 months of the books and stories you have read. Include the title, number of pages, and date read. Be prepared to tell your group about your favorite book or story.

405 Help build a doghouse, rabbit hutch, or chicken coop that is used by the animal or fowl. Keep a record of the cost, or the amount saved by using materials on hand.

406 Feed and care for chickens, fowl, or livestock for 1 month. Keep a record of the amount of time required.*

407 Help to run an incubator and hatch chickens successfully. Record cost and results.*

408 Figure out, for a week, the cost of each day's meals for your family. Do this with the help of an adult.

409 Make a listing of the speed limits for motor cars in different sections of your community. Know why they differ in different circumstances.

410 Follow a national event for 1 month by keeping newspaper clippings, reports of radio and television news, and magazine articles. Additional honor: Follow an international event, or a local or state topic.

411 Keep a group scrapbook for 1 month. Save programs, party favors, games, plans, publicity, etc.*

412 Help make a budget for your group, to include plan for national dues and purchase of group supplies.

413 Help make a budget for a group trip. Include cost of transportation, food, etc.

414 Help make a budget for a group camping trip; include costs of transportation, food, etc.

415 Keep an account of all the money spent for a group party or trip. List what was bought and the cost. Report expenses to your group.

Businesses

501 Visit a place of business to learn as much as you can about how this business operates. This may be a farm, an office, a store, a factory, a newspaper, a science laboratory, a museum.

502 Visit a bus or train station, airport or air terminal, or travel agency, to learn as much as you can about how this means of transportation operates to serve people.

503 Go on a tour through a hotel or motel to learn about the house-

keeping set-up, the services rendered, and how a guest should conduct herself. Do this with the cooperation of the management.

504 Attend an audition for your group at a local radio, television, or phonograph recording studio. Listen to your voices and make criticisms. Learn how this studio is operated.

505 Visit a local gas, electric, water, or telephone company. Request literature about its services. Ask questions about how it helps the community.

506 Visit a service or nonprofit organization to learn as much as you can about how this service serves people.

507 Learn about some of the state governmental services that are available to you and your family. Visit one with your group.

508 Visit your chamber of commerce and learn what it does. Write to the chamber of commerce in another city for literature about that city. Compare the two.

509 Learn about the Better Business Bureau: why it exists and how it functions.

Money and the Bank

601 Visit a bank. Have an official show you how the bank operates. Tell your family about the visit.

602 Learn how to open a savings account at a bank. Find out about deposits, withdrawals, and interest.

603 Make deposits in a savings account which you have opened, for at least 6 months.*

604 Learn how to make out and cash a check. Show how it should be endorsed, tell the procedure for stopping the payment on a check which has been lost, stolen, or made out incorrectly.

605 Learn how to check a bank statement, why keeping canceled checks is important, and how to file them.

606 Learn how to purchase travelers' checks. Learn the value of carrying money this way, the cost of checks, and in what way checks are cashed.

607 Find out what United States coins are made of, and where they are made.

608 Find out the denominations of United States paper money, and who signs it. Learn where it is made, and where new money is stored.

609 Learn whose picture is on a one, five, ten, twenty, and fifty dollar bill.

610 Learn the values of having a coin collection as a hobby, and what makes a coin become rare.

611 Visit a stock exchange and learn how it operates.

612 Learn what happens when you place an order for stock in a corporation.

The Post Office

701 Wrap and tie 3 packages for mailing: a box, a soft article, and a fragile article. Wrap 1 package as a gift. Do this with your group.

702 Prepare a package for shipping via parcel post or express. This should include addressing, and insurance.

703 Tour the post office with your group to learn about kinds of stamps, and their cost, different kinds of mailings, deliveries. Learn how citizens can help the postman and the post office department of your government. Find out who pays for the post office. Arrange this trip with the postmaster.

704 Using the Postal Guide, learn what type of mailing material is sent 1st class, 2nd class, 3rd class, 4th class, and how such material is to be wrapped and marked.

705 Learn and describe the postage rates for 1st class mail, 2nd class, 3rd class, 4th class, parcel post, special delivery, special handling, airmail, and postal rates to foreign countries.

706 Learn and show that you know how to read a postal scale, weighing mail to be sent by air, 1st, 2nd, 3rd, and 4th class mail.

707 Learn the different ways to purchase U.S. postage stamps, such as in small quantities, in sheets, books, and rolls of different sizes, or postal cards and stamped envelopes. How do the costs compare?

708 Learn about the dead letter office in your post office and how the post office traces lost mail.

709 Learn how to make out the proper form for a U.S. postal money order. Learn how to buy and pay for it, and how to cash it.

710 Learn the values of having a stamp collection as a hobby, and what makes a stamp rare.

711 Study a map showing the various zones. Learn zip code zones

for your area or city. Know why it is important to include the zip code number on letters.

Citizenship Craft

Myself

101 Wear your official Camp Fire service costume to 8 Camp Fire group meetings.*

102 Form a good habit by getting up in the morning the first time you are called, 5 times a week for 1 month.*

103 Have your blood typed, and record the type on wallet identification card.

104 Find out how fingerprints are taken and learn their importance as identification. As a group, take your own fingerprints and compare the different prints of each.

105 Be immunized or rechecked against polio, tetanus, or other diseases as recommended by your physician.*

106 Have a tuberculosis skin test. Follow this by X-ray if the test is positive.

107 Pretend you're a rag doll. Relax completely for at least 3 minutes twice a day for 2 weeks. Or, lie down for a nap 10 minutes a day for 2 weeks.*

108 Stand and sit tall; walk gracefully for a month. Watch your improvement.*

109 Make a list of some social graces which you would like to attain. Practice these and watch your improvement for 2 months.

110 Take care of your clothes. See that they are mended and clean. Put them in their proper place after wearing. Do this for a month.*

111 Offer your services to a shut-in or handicapped person for ½ hour, 3 times a week, for 2 weeks.*

112 Write a letter of appreciation to a public official or some person who has helped you in Camp Fire.

113 Read to, or write letters 4 different times for, someone who might welcome this service.*

My Family

201 Read chapters of this book with your mother or father. Continue this, at different times, until you have each looked through each chapter.

202 Hold at least 1 of your Camp Fire group meetings in your home, so that your family will have the opportunity of meeting your Camp Fire friends.

203 Think about your habits at home. Try for 1 month to correct a habit annoying to others, such as tuning radio too loud, using telephone too often and too long, etc.*

204 Correspond regularly for 6 months with a relative or friend.*

205 Make a family tree showing the names, countries, and occupations (if possible) of your grandparents and great grandparents.

206 Talk with some older person about the life and customs when he or she was young. Find out about clothes, manners, favorite activities, etc.

207 Plan and lead a family sing, party or other family get-together. Let each member of the family choose his or her favorite songs, games, or activities.

208 Encourage your family to use a bulletin board which you have made. Notes, reminders, and suggestions will go on it.

209 Use a suggestion box for a month, in which family members can place ideas for family fun.*

My Camp Fire Group and Other Friends

301 Give a party or have a hike for non-Camp Fire Girls who may be interested in joining your group or forming a new group.

302 Help a new or younger Camp Fire Girl to learn and understand the Camp Fire Girls Law and the Desires. Help her to choose her Camp Fire name and symbol.

303 Help a new or younger Camp Fire Girl to earn 3 honors.

304 Help to write and carry out an inspirational flag ceremony.

305 Help to plan and carry out a ceremonial on friendship.

306 Think of examples of friendship in a TV program, motion picture, a book, play, or real life. Discuss in your Camp Fire group what makes a good friend.

307 Help to plan and take part in a Mother-Daughter or Dad-Daughter event.

308 Make friends with an interesting adult (besides your guardian). Learn about his or her hobbies, and invite this person to a Camp Fire meeting that would be of special interest.

309 Have a party. Play games, make decorations, etc., to show the history and customs of the countries from which the ancestors of your group came. Know the contributions of these peoples to our country.

310 Visit an American antique show, fair, or exhibit with your group, or have an exhibit of heirlooms.

311 Work out and play in your group at least 3 times, 2 new Indian symbol games.

312 Tell a group at least 2 legends: include Asian, African, Indian etc.

313 Keep a list of all people who have helped your Camp Fire group. See that your group's appreciation is expressed in an appropriate way. Do this for 3 months.*

314 Arrange bulletin board or display which tells about Camp Fire Girls, for use at your school or library during Birthday Week or when new groups are being organized. Do this with your group.

315 Take part in a skit or give a talk about Camp Fire Girls. Do this at a public meeting or on radio or television.

316 Make decorations for a holiday, or individual gifts for patients in a home, or hospital. Present these at a time when your group can also entertain with carols or songs.

317 Take part in arranging and evaluating an exhibit supporting a community fund agency other than Camp Fire Girls.

318 Be a member of a committee in your group which plans with other children or adults, not connected with Camp Fire Girls, an activity which you will enjoy doing together.

319 Help your group make a layette for a new baby. Give it to an agency like the Needlework Guild or a community center.

320 Present a skit or play with your group which dramatizes some aspect of citizenship. This might be one of the Rights in the Bill of Rights or a new law.

My School

401 Invite 1 of your teachers to be your special guest at a Camp Fire meeting which you think she will enjoy.

402 Accompany a younger or handicapped child to and from school for 1 month.*

403 Discover how you can cooperate with the janitor or caretaker of the school or public library where your group meets. To learn this, invite the person to be your guest at a meeting.

404 Be a member of a group to help plan and carry out publicity for a ceremonial or some special Camp Fire program at school.

405 Make a plan with your Camp Fire group or with your class for ways in which you can make your school more attractive and friendly. With school approval, help to carry out your suggestions.

406 Have a responsible part in carrying out plans for a school carnival, hobby show, or exhibit.

407 Assist with a tea or other event for the parents of your schoolmates.

408 Help to plan and discuss safety measures suitable for your school. Decide how to use the best suggestions.

409 Be hostess to a newcomer in your school for 3 days, showing her about, introducing her to your friends, etc. Invite her to a Camp Fire group meeting.

410 Be a member of your school's Red Cross Youth and take an active part in its program for a school term.

411 Serve as traffic patrol for your school for the time appointed by your teacher.

412 Take a responsible part in keeping your schoolroom attractive, caring for plants, arranging bulletin boards, etc., or find some other way in which you can help your teacher regularly for 4 weeks.*

413 Show an improvement in your studies for 3 consecutive months.*

My Religion

501 Learn to sing 4 standard hymns (at least 2 verses) new to you.

502 Participate in the general worship services of your church or synagogue for 3 months.*

503 Attend, be on time, and share in religious education classes for your faith, for 3 consecutive months.*

504 Serve as an officer in some department or class in your church or synagogue and fulfill all the duties of office for 3 months.*

505 Give at least 10 per cent of your allowance or earnings to your church or synagogue for 3 months.*

506 Attend worship services different from your own with a friend. Do this with your parent's permission.

507 Read 5 stories about different religions. Discuss with your religious adviser the similarities to and differences from your religion.

508 Learn about the beliefs and practices of different churches in your community. Discuss these in your group.

509 Take part in daily family devotions in your home, for 1 month.*

510 Plan and participate in a devotional service at camp or when your group is camping together.

511 Participate in a skit or other part of the program for family night at your place of worship.

512 Give 10 hours of service to your church or religous organization, by helping with clerical work, addressing envelopes, folding letters, running the mimeograph machine, etc.*

513 Attend all rehearsals and sing regularly in a choir for a period of time agreed upon by your parents and the director.*

514 Read a different chapter from the Bible or other religious literature every day for 1 month. (Follow suggestions made by your religious adviser.)*

515 Go on a conducted tour of some large church, cathedral, synagogue, or religious shrine.

516 Help in a nursery 4 times, in order that parents may be free to attend worship services.*

517 Help to provide and arrange the flowers for your place of worship 4 times.*

518 Help to clean the silver and/or brass at your place of worship 3 times.*

519 Give 5 hours of service in helping to mend and repair torn prayer books, or church school books.

520 Give 5 hours of service to your place of worship, such as helping to clean, dust, put meeting rooms in order, etc.*

521 Assist in the church library for 5 hours.*

522 Contribute service to a foreign or home mission program, such as collecting clothing, packing, sewing, earning funds, or giving funds out of your own money.

523 Participate in a service project new to you which is recommended by your church or synagogue.

524 Take an active part in a brotherhood project sponsored by organizations in your community to promote better interreligious and interracial understanding.

My Community

601 Form a good habit: do not throw papers or other litter on the street out of car windows, or on the ground at camp or other places, for 2 months.*

602 Arrange a Treasure Hike or an Exploration Hike in your own neighborhood.

603 Have a country or square dance evening for your neighbors.

604 Help to plan and take part in a neighborhood hobby or treasure show.

605 See a different neighborhood through a visit to another Camp Fire group in another section of your town.

606 Collect information about interesting trips you have taken with your group or your family.

607 Make a map of the government and historical buildings and/or parks in your community. Illustrate and color.

608 Help with a community tree or flower-planting project.

609 Make some definite contribution to your community by beautifying yards, practicing conservation or protection of trees, or taking care in the matter of rubbish and fire hazards.

610 Take part in the planning or celebration of a historical event of local significance.

611 Be a member of a group which is carrying out the celebration of a national holiday, such as Independence Day.

612 Do the same for a Health Day or other community event.

613 Be a member of a group which plans and carries out a successful winter carnival or spring festival for the community. Take an active part in the work and planning.

614 Take part in a community Christmas tree celebration, either indoors or out.*

615 Go caroling at holiday time. Sing at the homes of shut-ins, at hospitals, or at some public spot.

616 Arrange with your local postmaster or newspaper to answer Santa Claus letters.*

617 Make a May basket, fill it with flowers and/or cookies or candy, and take it to a shut-in.

618 Send a card or letter to a shut-in each week for 2 months.*

619 Help to provide toys or books for the children's ward of a local hospital.*

620 Find out what is needed by a hospital, convalescent home or children's institution. Discuss these suggestions with your group and choose a project and carry it out.

621 Give a dramatic or musical entertainment with your group, for a hospital, children's institution or other welfare organization.*

622 Help in a United Fund drive by making your own contribution, filling envelopes, distributing posters, ushering, etc.

623 Visit a health or welfare agency and find out about its services. Arrange for your visit in advance.

624 Visit the library to find out how it is managed; learn how to use a card catalog, readers' guides, and something about the arrangement and distribution of books.

625 Invite a new neighbor or friend to go to the library with you. Help her to become acquainted with it and to take out a card.

626 Mend and repair books or manuscripts for a library, play center, or reading room.

627 Help start a camp library or contribute to a library a new book bought with your own money.

628 Take a visitor in the community to your library, museum, or other public place in your city.

629 Visit the courthouse of your county and observe the legal activities carried on there. In advance, invite a lawyer or judge to tell your group what to look for.

630 Take part in a visit to a water purification plant. Learn the dangers of water-borne diseases, the uses of water in your community, and the methods used for purifying water.

631 Visit a police station, a police academy, and/or the jail to learn how policemen enforce the law.

632 Learn how your community provides and manages 1 service that your family enjoys, such as fire and police protection, traffic control, sanitation, water supply, public schools, etc. Visit at least 1 place where such service originates.

633 Learn what you can do in your community to correct and prevent pollution, and carry it out.

634 Attend a session where your local laws or ordinances are made.

635 Find out about careers in public service in your community. Learn what these people do to serve you, and interview one to inquire about his or her specific job.

My State and Country

701 Add 3 new words about your state or country to your vocabulary. Tell your group their meaning.

702 Make a pictorial map of your state to show historical points and to locate interesting places.

703 Go through the Capitol and 2 other public buildings in the capital city of your state. Think of questions beforehand which you will want to have answered. Have a guide with you; make a report to your group or your family.

704 Find out some of the state governmental services that are available to you and your family. Visit one.

705 Find out when your state was admitted to the Union and which star of the flag represents it.

706 Learn what you can about your state flag and how it is displayed with our national flag.

707 Start a scrapbook containing souvenirs of visits to at least 5 historical buildings, monuments, or shrines.

708 Get a map and information about state or national parks in your state. Visit one and tell what accommodations and advantages it offers tourist or camper, and how it is maintained.

709 Tell your group the stories of at least 1 great man and 1 great woman who have emigrated to America.

710 Tell of at least 3 important events in American history affecting the status of women.

711 Tell the history and meaning of the Flag of the United States of America.

712 Lead a group in the Pledge of Allegiance to the Flag of the United States of America. Demonstrate the rules for display and care of the flag. Give the date for Flag Day.

713 Take responsibility for displaying the U.S. flag in your home for 3 national holidays.

714 Learn the Star Spangled Banner and the story of how it came to be written.

715 Learn all the verses of "America" and "America the Beautiful."

716 Name the author and composer of a great American patriotic song. Describe how it was written, or write a skit on this subject and act it out.

717 Learn the Bill of Rights and illustrate one part. Use photographs, magazine pictures, newspaper articles.

718 Write the group's "Bill of Responsibilities," with other members of your group. Relate it to the Bill of Rights and the Camp Fire Girls Law.

719 Go through the Capitol and 2 other public buildings in Washington, D.C. Have a guide; make a report to your family or your group.

720 Find out who represents your state in the United States Senate and House of Representatives. Report on this to your group.

721 Read 2 books that help you understand the contribution of different national or racial groups who make up the U.S.

722 Have a fashion show or make an exhibit of the dress or costumes which reflect different periods of our national history.

723 Collect 5 foreign stamps commemorating events in United States history, and/or 5 foreign stamps which honor great Americans. Learn something about these people.

724 Attend a ceremony at which people are made U.S. citizens. With your group help plan a special welcome for these new citizens.

725 Learn how citizens register to vote and the voting procedures in your state.

726 Help distribute non-partisan literature on candidates and issues before an election. Do this in cooperation with a group such as the League of Women Voters.

727 Start or add to your collection of American stamps. Show it to a group, and tell them something of the history of at least 5 stamps.

728 Know some of the historical background of at least 5 coins in your coin collection.

729 Sing 3 genuine American Indian songs from memory, alone or with a group.

730 Learn about the Indian tribes which originally inhabited your state, the tribes and number of members now living there, their background and economic condition.

731 Name, and visit if possible, the Indian tribe which originally lived

nearest your section of the state. Find out about their symbolism, hand arts, and how they live today.

732 Explain to new members of your group why the founders of Camp Fire Girls were interested in Indian lore and why much of the beauty and symbolism of Indian lore was put into the program.

733 Find out which Indian tribe is known for: katchina dolls, totem poles, tepees, hogans, pueblos, longhouses.

734 Demonstrate 15 signs of Indian handsign language.

735 Describe or act out at least three methods used by Indian tribes to communicate with one another.

736 Visit one of the following: an Indian Mission, museum, school or reservation; an Indian ruin, battleground, national monument or state event. Tell someone about your visit.

737 Learn what is being done by the government today for the welfare of the Indians.

738 Be a working member of a group to help collect Indian legends. Record them with illustrations.

739 Select at least 5 examples or pictures of costumes, moccasins, baskets, pottery, weaving or other hand arts of Indians from different sections of your country. Label them with name of tribe, state, etc. Find out what you can about how they were made.

740 Describe a genuine Indian ceremony or festival which you have seen; tell about its tribe, its meaning, and how it is celebrated.

741 Mark on a map of your state 8 or 10 rivers, cities, or other geographical areas which have Indian names. Discover the tribes from which these names were taken. If possible, tell the English meaning.

742 Learn about the lives and activities of 3 well-known Indians, men or women. Share your knowledge with a group of friends or your Camp Fire group.

Our World

801 Arrange a meeting and invite a neighbor or friend from another country to talk about the customs, people, folk history, etc., of her country.

802 Have a food-of-all-nations fair with your group. Invite people from other countries to assist you in planning. This might be

a group money-making affair for some service project you want to carry out for children of other lands.

803 Plan a celebration of a holiday as it is celebrated in another land. Entertain your friends, explaining the holiday to them.

804 Learn how 5 other countries give thanks for a bountiful harvest. Make at least 3 of the ideas a part of your group or personal Thanksgiving celebration.

805 Learn the date and significance of United Nations Day and of 1 national holiday of each of 3 foreign countries.

806 Be a member of a group which plans and carries out an observance of United Nations Day.

807 Tour the United Nations headquarters, and if possible attend a meeting of the General Assembly or other body. Give a report on this.

808 Read the Preamble to the United Nations Charter, and explain how the Camp Fire Girls program helps to carry out the principles of world friendship.

809 Learn to speak and write correctly at least 10 useful phrases in another language.

810 Take part in making a group exhibit of model dwellings, past and present, lived in by people in different parts of the world. This could include trees, wigwams, tree houses, adobe houses, thatched houses, skyscrapers, etc.

811 Learn about flags of 3 foreign countries. Share models or illustrations with your group and discuss the correct display of foreign flags.

812 Follow 1 world event in newspapers for 1 month; clip all the articles you find, and present a summary of the event in your Camp Fire meeting.*

813 Contribute 5 hours of volunteer service to an organization which aids some other country.*

814 Give a talk on another country to your group, based on your personal travel experiences. Illustrate with exhibit or pictures, if possible.

815 Show 5 foreign portrait stamps and explain why these people were important to the history of their country and ours.

816 Collect post cards from 5 different countries and tell interesting facts about each.

817 Read 2 books that help you understand people of other nations.

818 Visit the Pan American Union or some other international center in Washington, D.C. Tell your group about your visit and some of the interesting facts you learned.

Creative Arts Craft

Hand Arts

DESIGNING AND PAINTING

101 Make a drawing suitable for a repeat design. Use straight lines and curves.

102 Finger paint and mount a painting of a personal feeling (how you feel about something).

103 Make a picture using colored sand or salt. Or paint a picture using sponge in place of a brush.

104 Make a picture using torn colored construction paper, or using string and paint.

105 Spatter 3 or more designs, using at least 2 colors. Or do at least 3 blow paintings, using ink or water color or both.

106 Make at least 1 chalk drawing. Use any of the following methods: chalk on rough paper, wet paper, or dipped in buttermilk.

107 Decorate an object with paint using a folk design of another land.

108 Draw or paint a landscape, seascape, buildings, or street scene.

109 Make at least 3 ink sketches on moistened paper.

110 Make sketches in 3 different media, such as crayon, water color pencil, charcoal, chalk, pastel, oil paint, or water color.

111 Paint a picture expressing rhythm and colors suggested by music, poetry, literature, or a personal feeling.

112 Paint a picture of a trip or an experience that impressed you.

113 Participate in an outdoor or indoor art show, displaying the drawings, sketches and hand art articles made by you and your group.

114 Make and decorate one of these: a washable cover for a cookbook, a bound recipe collection, 12 labels for food containers, or a family bulletin board.

115 Make a traditional folk or holiday decoration, such as a Christmas crèche, decorated Easter eggs, a Hannukah top, or menorah.

116 Blow out the contents of several eggs. Decorate the shells, using paint, crayon, glue and glitter, cut paper designs. Hang them by threads to make a mobile and use as party or holiday decorations.

117 Design and make greeting cards, wrapping paper, package trimming, or ornaments.

118 Make any holiday decorations for a party, by wrapping string dipped in paste, or liquid starch around balloons.

119 Decorate a window for a shut-in. Use tempera paint with a pinch of detergent or hang up colored tissue designs. Remove decorations and clean the window at an agreed upon time.

120 Make and/or paint or decorate a piece of furniture, equipment or game for outdoor use. This might be a bird house, a bird bath, or a lawn sign.

121 Paint, decorate, or redecorate one of the following: a chair, cabinet, knife rack, canister set, bread box, cheese board, tray, set of coasters, or any other piece of kitchen equipment.

122 Draw and cut out a paper doll that looks like you in proportion and coloring. Make 3 dresses for her.

123 Help plan and make a wall decoration such as a mural for your home, for a community room, or for an exhibit.

124 Help to arrange for a Family Art Gallery to display your family's creative efforts, and keep it up to date for 2 months or more.

125 Help prepare for and set up a Camp Fire Girls display, exhibit or demonstration.*

126 Make a picture scrapbook for a shut-in or child care center. Use original sketches or cartoons.

PAPER AND PRINT MAKING

201 Make 2 paper articles such as hats, masks, or aprons to be used at a party. Decorate with paint, crayon, raffia, yarn, etc.

202 Decorate paper to be used as a wall or window hanging or place mat. Use print, batik with rubber cement, crayons or wax.

203 Decorate paper for use as gift wrapping. Use paint, batik with rubber cement, crayons, or wax.

204 Shape an article of papier mâché or pulp, such as a dish, holiday

ornament, or puppet head. Decorate with paint or cut paper, gummed seals, or paper punch mosaics.

205 Make kitchen prints, using such forms as bottle tops, potato mashers, wooden or metal forks or spoons, tin cans, jars, etc.

206 Cut a design on a potato, carrot, or green pepper, and use for block printing.

207 Cut simple symbol designs out of felt, inner tubing, or sponge. Mount on blocks; use them to print an all-over pattern.

208 Prepare or make party trimmings, such as invitations, favors, place cards, placemats, napkins, decorated paper plates, score cards for games.

209 Make a doll house, trains, a village, automobiles or buses, or anything else you can think of, out of empty cardboard boxes. Give to a child.

TEXTILE ARTS

301 Make, line and equip a sewing box to hold your sewing supplies (scissors, pins, needles, thread, thimble, pin cushion, tape measure, etc.)

302 Learn to sew buttons, hooks and eyes, and snaps onto your own clothes.

303 Adjust the hem of a skirt, using slip-stitching.

304 Use 3 or 4 basic sewing stitches to decorate a fabric article such as a bookmark, belt, beanbag, needlebook.

305 Learn how to thread and care for a sewing machine.

306 Collect samples of at least 6 different fabrics used in sewing, and learn about their special qualities.

307 Learn to machine-stitch a straight line and a curve, to turn corners and end off.

308 Make a simple article such as an apron or scarf.

309 Make or decorate a tote bag for a handicapped or elderly person.

310 Make 3 dish towels, a 4-piece set of doilies, 2 place mats and napkins, or 3 pot holders.

311 Make an outfit for a doll.

312 Make 3 articles for a baby. This could be part of the Needlework Guild of America project.

313 Make 2 doll's outfits, washable stuffed toys or a child's garment, or 3 bibs for a child.

314 Make an original design. Embroider and/or appliqué it on such items as napkins, place mats, aprons, small table cloths, baby blankets, wall hangings.

315 Embroider or weave a design on net or stiff canvas; or work a design in needle point or petit point on an article such as a bag, belt, book cover, etc.

316 Use a simple weave to make an article such as a mat, basket, or sit-upon.

317 Use a cardboard, peg-type, soda straw, flat frame, or Indian-type loom to weave an article.

318 Use one of the above looms to make an article with natural materials such as cane, straw, reed, grass, fronds, etc.

319 Knit on a spool an article such as a pot holder, a mat, or a bag.

320 Knit or crochet 4 squares for an afghan, or 2 articles for a small child. This could be part of the Needlework Guild of America project.

321 Braid and knot cord to make articles such as a belt, bag, or lanyard.

322 Design and/or make a small hooked, braided, crocheted or woven rug, mat, or wall hanging.

Modeling, Shaping, Casting, Carving

401 Visit a pottery. See the potter at work. Observe the potter's wheel and kiln.

402 Design and make an attractive piece of pottery.

403 Model jewelry, dish, figure, doll or puppet head, mask or holiday decorations out of salt dough, sawdust clay, papier-mâché, or other clay-like powder or pulp mixtures.

404 Make a plaster cast in sand of an imprint you have discovered or a shape you have scooped out.

405 Make a figure, a head, or jewelry using self-hardening clay, casting, carving clay or plaster.

406 Dip string or clothesline in plaster, drop on wax paper and quickly form into a desired shape.

407 Make 3 candles by the dipping process or by pouring liquid wax in a mold.

408 Model or carve a shape or figure out of floating white soap, wax, paraffin, blocks of melted-together crayon or balsa wood.

409 Combine colored tissue and wire to form a mobile or a stabile.

410 Form and shape soft wire into the shape of a person, symbol, flower, animal, etc.

411 Make a mask, animal, or other form, using crushed aluminum foil, or foil over papier mâché.

412 Create a figure by combining materials such as bark, twigs, seed pods and cellophane.

413 Make a sculpture using branches, stumps, gnarled roots, driftwood, stones, or fungus.

Working with Wood, Glass, Plastic, Metals, Leather

501 Decorate a wooden article or gourd with paint, carving, batik, nature materials, or other.

502 Make a wall decoration by fastening together an assemblage of pieces of wood and foam rubber.

503 Use wood and/or foam rubber to make a simple toy or game. This could be a jumping jack, a pull toy, a jointed puppet, a train, or a jigsaw puzzle. Decorate with color.

504 Make and/or decorate a fireplace brush, wood box, footstool, shelves, bookends, plant or flower holder.

505 Make a stained glass window decoration, using pieces of colored plastic, X-ray film, or cellophane.

506 Use tile, glass, plastic, or leather to make a mosaic decoration.

507 Make a holiday wreath of wire. Decorate with materials such as glass, plastic, or metal.

508 Use coat hanger wire or other flexible wire to form wire figures. Suspend them or mount on blocks.

509 Use scrap metal and wire to form jewelry or a household article. These may be decorated with bits of wire, tin, glass or stones.

510 Make a piece of caged jewelry; wrap stone or glass in copper, brass, or silver wire.

511 Decorate a plastic or glass article with an etched, laminated, carved, pierced, or painted design.

512 Decorate a metal article with stippling, piercing, etching, liquid plastic, or fired enamel.

513 Make a simple leather article such as a lapel pin, coin purse, billfold, belt, bookmark. Decorate with a symbol or other design.

514 Make a wind harp.

Symbolism

601 Make a totem pole either by carving it or by using cardboard boxes.

602 Carve and decorate a katchina doll.

603 Use nature materials such as beans, peas, lentils and rice, to design a symbolgram.

604 Use symbols to decorate a sports item such as a ball, beach umbrella, cap and bag, jacket, paddle.

605 Make a symbol transparency, using colored tissue paper, melted crayons, construction paper and sheets of wax paper.

606 Make a flag, pennant, banner or mural for your group meeting room. Decorate it with your group symbol.

607 Develop a pictograph or symbol story on large cardboard, paper or cloth. Color it with paint, crayons, cut paper, or use nature materials.

608 Help make a felt board and a set of 20-25 symbols. Use these to try out decorations, symbolgrams for your ceremonial costumes, to tell symbol stories, or to help another group learn about symbols.

609 Make a symbol corsage or symbol-decorated gift to present to a guest of honor on a special occasion. Explain the meaning of the symbols.

610 Make your own personal felt board on the inside cover of a box, and a set of Indian symbols to show how you make symbolgrams, or to tell a symbol story.

611 Collect 20 or more everyday symbols: historic, patriotic, insignia, flags, traffic, weather, map-making, trade-marks, cattle brands. Draw or mount pictures of these to show your group, or to help another group learn symbols.

612 Show contrast in designs, illustrations or symbols, in a collection of about 20 old-fashioned and 20 modern greeting cards, valentines, book jackets, sheet music covers or calendars.

613 Make something you will wear in ceremonials, such as a belt or bracelet of honor bead jewelry, a headband, or moccasins. Decorate with your symbolgram.

614 Make and decorate with symbols something you will use in ceremonials. This may be a sit-upon, a case for your ceremonial

costume and beads, candle snuffer, ceremonial chest, candle board.

615 Decorate your ceremonial gown with leather collar and border designs. Use your symbolgram.

The Dance

701 Attend a dance performance given by professional, or skilled amateur, dancers.

702 Listen to 3 well-known ballets on records. Tell a brief story of each.

703 Help secure a film on the dance from a film library or a university, to show to your group and others.

704 Learn to dance a folk dance of another country. Explain the traditions relating to the dance.

705 Take part in folk dances which your group performs before an audience.

706 Learn 2 American Indian tribal dances.

707 Tell a story by means of pantomime or dancing.

708 Do a "yes" and "no" dance pantomime, showing how Camp Fire Girls should act in various situations.

709 Demonstrate running, marching, skipping, and leaping, to music. Help choose the appropriate music for each. Do this outdoors or indoors.

710 Interpret in dance movements 3 things you see in nature, such as the movements of trees, birds, water, clouds.

711 Listen to different kinds of music. Try to express in physical movement the moods and ideas they suggest: sadness, joy, etc.

712 Make up a dance to dramatize an important event.

713 Make up a dance to music you like.

714 Make up a dance that will tell a story, paint a picture, or describe a mood or feeling.

715 Design a dance to accompany choral speaking.

716 Make up a dance depicting a part of Camp Fire Girls lore.

717 Make up a dance to folk music, using traditional folk dance steps.

718 Help teach 1 or 2 folk dances to a younger group.

719 Help teach younger children 6 or more dance steps.

720 Practice good posture exercises so important in dancing, for a few minutes each day for 1 month.*

721 Take dancing lessons. Practice at least half an hour daily for 1 month.*

Music

801 Attend a concert or musical program. Find out as much as you can beforehand about the music you will hear.

802 Take one of your favorite records to a "music meeting" of your group. Tell why you like it. Help the group to sing with it, or to make up a dance or pantomime to it.

803 Plan and give a program of records and prepare program notes for your guests.

804 Demonstrate how to use and care for a record player, including the needle. Show how to handle and store your records.

805 Carefully clean, catalog, and arrange your own or your family's record collection; or do this for someone else.

806 Sing or play at least 5 songs written for Camp Fire Girls.

807 Sing 5 folk songs from different countries. Do this with others.

808 Learn two American Indian lullabies, rhythms, songs or chants.

809 Play 1 selection from an opera for the pleasure of a group, telling the story of the opera selected.

810 Teach your group to sing a song you learned at camp.

811 Tune glasses and play a melody on them, using a tapper you have made yourself.

812 Make and decorate a drum, tambourine, marimba or other instrument, and play it in a rhythm orchestra.

813 Accompany your group singing with a musical instrument. Do this 4 times.*

814 Make up a Camp Fire Girls song or a hiking song.

815 Help make up a theme song for your group.

816 Learn without the help of your teacher to play or sing any musical number well enough to present it for the pleasure of others.

817 Learn 5 bugle calls to play at camp.

818 Take part in a "human-a-phone" program with your group. Help make the props.

819 Participate in a performance with a choral group.*

820 Participate in a musical festival. This could be during National Music Week.

821 Have an International Folk Festival in costume. Sing, play, or dramatize your favorite folk songs and dances. Make decorations featuring the folk art of the various countries chosen.

822 Practice at least half an hour daily on a musical instrument (or voice) for 1 month.*

Dramatics

901 Make and decorate one of the following types of masks: paper bag, paper box, cylinder, cloth, papier mâché, or large paper plate mask. Use it in a play, pageant, game or party.

902 Make at least 4 cardboard finger puppets. Show your group how they are used.

903 Make any of the following puppets, to present to another child or use in a show: fingerette, spoon or ladle puppet, fist, sock, bib, cut paper and rod, or peanut puppet.

904 Make a jointed cardboard string puppet or a paper bag puppet.

905 Present a puppet you have made to a child. Give a show with it first.

906 Make a simple cardboard box stage and scenery for a puppet show. Use it to give a show, and/or present it with puppets as a gift.

907 Make a peep show, or shadow box show. Show it to your group and tell them how you made it.

908 Act out a story or personal experience for your group from an outline you have made. Rehearse it carefully first, paying particular attention to speaking, gestures, and posture.

909 Act out a story. Do this alone or with others.

910 Interpret a poem or poems for others.

911 Read for your group 1 act of a short play. Change your voice quickly from one character to the next.

912 Help plan and give an entertainment such as shadow play, talent show, pantomime, charades, or skit.

913 Take part in a choral speaking production for a public performance.

914 Start a costume box to be used for informal dramatics. Include a make-up kit.

915 Be an active member of a school or community dramatic club, or a little theater group.

916 Take lessons in dramatics, public speaking, or corrective speech. Practice daily for the time recommended by your instructor for 1 month.*

Creative Writing

1001 Write an account of your group's activities in poetry or prose. Read it at a group ceremonial.

1002 Write a one-act play suitable for 2 puppet characters.

1003 Write a short play based on an experience, real or imaginary.

1004 Write a story or article on the Law of the Camp Fire Girls. Tell what it means to you and your family.

1005 Write an original poem or a candle lighting ceremony which is used in a group ceremonial.

1006 Contribute to a group scrapbook at least 4 bits of poetry or prose you have written or collected, to be used in group ceremonials.*

1007 See the movie of a book you have read, and discuss with your group or your family the differences between the two.

1008 Have a book party. Dress as your favorite character, author, or illustrator. Plan games around books. Invite guests if you wish. Act out or pantomime your character.

1009 Set aside time 3 times a week for a month to write letters, some poetry, or prose. (This should be other than school assignments.) Share with an adult friend.*

Home Craft

A Good Housekeeper

101 Plan an arrangement for your belongings, and keep them in order for 1 month.*

102 Plan a neat arrangement for your closet; make a permanent place for clothes, shoes, etc. Keep it in order for 1 month.*

103 Make a list of things you should do that need to be done daily, weekly, monthly, etc., to keep your room clean. Check it with an adult. Note the items you can do yourself.

104 Discuss with family members ways in which everyone can co-operate to keep your home neat and attractive. Make a list of things you will do to help.

105 Listen to 3 recommended radio or TV programs related to home-making, such as cooking, marketing, etc.

106 Keep a room neat and clean for 1 month.*

107 Keep woodwork clean in 2 rooms for 1 month.*

108 Start a kitchen scrapbook, a file of household hints, new and/or favorite recipes, or party ideas, etc.

109 Learn about the cleaning and laundry products used in your home. Use 3.

110 Clean and wax a small floor.

111 Learn to polish metals in your home such as copper, aluminum, stainless steel, silver. Polish several objects.

112 Use and care for a vacuum cleaner in your home 3 times. Empty the bag.

113 Learn to use the vacuum attachments to an adult's satisfaction.

114 Empty all the garbage and trash containers in your home for a 2-week period.*

115 Help carry in wood for the fireplace. Lay the fire on 3 occasions and clean the fireplace afterwards.

116 Wash or dry dishes and leave the dining room and kitchen in order after 1 meal a day for 1 week. Two girls may share this, continuing it for twice the time.*

117 Learn about the use and care of cooking utensils in your kitchen.

118 Learn about the use and care of small appliances in your kitchen.

119 Choose one small appliance or utensil, such as an electric fry pan, 2-quart sauce pan, electric broiler or rotisserie. Learn about the different types of foods that can be cooked in it, and prepare one dish.

120 Defrost and clean a refrigerator, and learn where certain foods should be stored, such as milk, butter, meats, eggs, vegetables, frozen foods, etc.

121 Keep the top of the kitchen range clean for 1 month.

122 Clean the oven twice with an adult supervising.

123 Improve the efficiency of your kitchen in at least 1 way, with your family's approval. Examples: save motions and steps in setting the table, in unpacking and storing groceries. Store equipment nearest spot of use.

124 Load and operate a washing machine and/or drier. Take proper care of the equipment afterwards.

125 Do 6 pieces of hand washing.

126 Help fold, sort, and put away family laundry 4 times.*

127 Learn to use an electric iron, and iron the small flat pieces of the family's laundry.

128 Iron or press 6 items of clothing.

129 Learn how to press or iron wool, silk, rayon, linens, embroidery, and synthetic materials.

130 Help prepare clothing for seasonal storage.

131 Learn at least 4 ways in which you can conserve water in your own home. Put them into practice for 4 weeks.*

Food Preparation

201 Prepare 4 different milk drinks or milk shakes.

202 Prepare 6 different fruit drinks or coolers.

203 Prepare 6 sandwiches you have never tried before.

204 Prepare a hamburger dish 4 different ways.

205 Make 3 kinds of salads you and your friends will enjoy.

206 Prepare 4 different vegetables.

207 Prepare eggs, cheese, or fish as the main dish of a meal.

208 Prepare a main course in one of the following ways: boiled, broiled, baked, one-dish, cold plate, braise, fry.

209 Take 3 different convenience foods and prepare a dish from each.

210 Cook 3 of the following in 3 main dishes: corn meal, dried beans, dried peas, hominy, lentils, rice, noodles, macaroni, spaghetti.

211 Prepare a soup from a standard recipe.

212 Make 2 of the following twice, once using standard recipes and once using mixes: biscuits, griddle cakes, rolls, waffles, popovers, muffins, yeastbreads. Compare cost and taste of the mix and the standard recipe.

213 Use fruit in 3 different desserts.

214 Make 3 kinds of cookies, such as rolled, drop, refrigerator. Use a mix or frozen dough for one kind if you wish.

215 Make 2 kinds of puddings from a standard recipe.

216 Make a pudding or gelatin mix 4 times, each with a different recipe.

217 Make a cake twice from a standard recipe.

218 Make a cake 4 times with a mix.

219 Make a frosting twice with a standard recipe. Frost cakes or a cake which you have made.

220 Make a frosting 4 times from mixes, to frost cup cakes or a cake which you have made.

221 Make pie crusts twice, using standard recipes.

222 Make pie crusts 4 times, using a mix.

223 Make 2 kinds of candy.

224 Make 2 kinds of frozen desserts.

225 Cook 1 meal a day for a week. Remember to include foods from the Basic Four groups.

226 Plan, prepare, and pack a lunch for yourself or for someone in your family, every school or working day for 2 weeks. Be sure you include the foods needed from the Basic Four groups.*

227 Plan, prepare, and serve 2 meals (1 a dinner) for your family, relieving adults of all the responsibility. Be sure you include the foods needed from the Basic Four groups.*

228 Help with cooking a meal a day for 1 month.*

229 Prepare and serve 3 of the recipes in honor #302.

230 Collect 5 recipes from each of 4 foreign countries. Prepare and serve to your family 1 recipe from each country.

231 Choose one country from honor #230. Learn all you can about how the people live and eat in that country. Prepare and serve a meal as it would be done in that country.

232 Ask someone who has lived in another country to teach you how to cook some dish known to that country. Bring the recipe or a sample to Camp Fire meeting.

233 Go to a fruit and vegetable store and make a list of all the fruits and all the vegetables sold there. If there are some you have never seen before, find out what they are and how they are prepared or served.

234 Prepare and serve 2 fruits, vegetables, or meats you have never tried before.

235 Learn how food is produced, by visiting such places as a dairy, a farm, a freezing plant, a cannery, or a food factory.

236 Invite a nutritionist or home economist to speak to your group. Prepare questions to ask her about food and cooking.

237 Learn the correct way to store vegetables, like onions and potatoes, which are not kept in the refrigerator. Check to be sure they are stored this way in your home.

238 Find out 5 ways to package food for the freezer. Learn the correct way to package each kind of food: fruits, vegetables or meat.

239 Prepare and freeze 3 quarts of fruit or vegetables.

240 Package and freeze 1 kind of raw meat.

241 Package and freeze food you have prepared, such as a casserole, bread or rolls, a pie or a cake.

242 Make 1 quart of pickles or relish.

243 Make 4 glasses of jam, or a fruit butter like apple butter.

244 Can 4 jars of fruit or vegetables, using method recommended by your State Extension Service. If you can vegetables other than tomatoes, you must use a pressure canner.

245 Visit a freezing plant or canning factory to see how food is preserved commercially.

Note: For Shopping and Purchasing honors, see Business Craft.

Meal Planning

301 Start your own collection of recipes. Use them in earning Home Craft honors.

302 Collect 10 recipes from other parts of the United States. Learn where they are from and something about each area.

303 Learn the Basic Four food groups. Name 10 foods from each group.

304 List everything you eat for 3 days. Check with the Basic Four chart. See if you have eaten the kinds of foods you need each day. Make a list of other things you could eat to make your meals better.

305 Plan and eat a balanced breakfast every day for 4 weeks, which includes: fruit or fruit juice, cocoa or milk, an egg 3 to 5 days and cereal on other days, toast or muffins.*

306 Plan Basic Four lunches for 5 days.

307 Eat a lunch every day based on 1 of the menus planned in honor #306. When you have done this for 1 month you have earned this honor.*

308 Keep a Rosy Cheeks Diary for 1 month.*

Hostess Skills

401 Entertain one or more friends in your home for 3 afternoons.

402 Prepare your bedroom for an overnight guest.

403 Plan recreation for the children of your mother's visitors.

404 Prepare a favorite family recipe.

405 Plan and cook a balanced breakfast for the family.

406 Set the table attractively for 1 meal, 5 days a week for a month.*

407 Plan and arrange a timely centerpiece for your family's table on 2 occasions.

408 Learn the ways coffee and tea are prepared and served to guests in your home.

409 Prepare an appetizing and attractive meal in which the main dishes are made from left-overs.

410 Plan, prepare, and serve an attractive birthday meal for a member of your family.

411 Plan, prepare, and serve a meal twice for a friend or friends.

412 Help plan and make arrangements for a party marking a special family occasion.

413 Plan table decorations and favors for a party.

414 Write invitations, acceptances, or thank-yous for 3 different kinds of social situations, such as a party, a tea, a house guest or a meal.

415 Have someone speak to your group on the responsibilities of hostess and guest.

416 Invite guests to your home to hear or see a Camp Fire Girls broadcast on radio or TV. Furnish each one with a postal card. Ask them to write their appreciation to the broadcasting station.

417 Be a co-hostess for a party in another person's home or meeting place.

418 Learn to play a game enjoyed by an older person when he or she was a child. Teach it to your Camp Fire group.

419 Help to have a party for the parents of the girls in your group.

420 Have a Camp Fire Girls family party with a Dads' Cake Making Contest. Or, think of another contest. Have judges, simple prizes, "samples," games, fun.

421 Help your group give a party for another group of girls. This includes planning, invitations, decorations, food preparation and serving.

422 Plan a birthday party for a pre-school child. Make and/or decorate the birthday cake. Help lead games.

423 Have a party for children in a hospital or other institution. Have your plans approved beforehand by the hospital staff.

424 Make a gift to give to your host or hostess.

Natural Beauty

501 Keep the outdoor areas and entries to your home free from litter for 2 months.*

502 Learn the names of 15 plants or shrubs whose names you do not know, by walking around your neighborhood or visiting a florist or public garden.

503 Learn about 7 plants or shrubs commonly grown in your area: when they are planted, when they bloom or bear fruit, how to care for them, appearance at different seasons, how high they grow, etc.

504 Accompany your family to a garden supply center and learn all you can about what is sold there.

505 Learn the use of all garden tools and supplies in your home. Practice using 2 of them.

506 Have a collection of 4 kinds of house plants, or herbs grown indoors. Care for it without assistance for a season.*

507 Plant a window or porch box. Maintain it in good condition for an entire season.*

508 Grow 3 or more kinds of vegetables from seed.

509 Plant 6 bulbs for outdoor blooming, or for indoor blooming, or for blooming in window boxes.*

510 Grow from seed 6 or more kinds of annuals, perennials, or plants from slips. Do all the work yourself; preparing soil, planting, cultivating, weeding, watering, protecting from insects or disease.*

511 Plan, plant, and care for a small garden for a season. This may be a rock, cactus, fern, herb, wild flower, water, or other kind.*

512 Give flowers from your garden to a shut-in or your family 3 times.*

513 Attend a flower show. Give a talk to your group about it.

514 Invite a gardener or someone from a flower shop or garden club to talk with your group about gardening or flower arranging.

515 Enter for exhibit a plant, flower, or vegetable specimen you have grown yourself.*

516 Enter for exhibit an arrangement of flowers, plants or vegetables.*

517 Plan and have a garden show with your group. Invite special guests.

518 Assist in family garden care work of any kind, 2 hours each week for 2 months.*

519 Learn to recognize the weeds in your yard, lawn, or garden, and help keep it weeded for 2 months.

520 Take responsibility for sprinkling your family's lawn during 2 hot weeks.*
521 Help prepare a garden or yard for a new season. Spend at least 3 hours.*
522 Plant and care for a tree for 1 season.

Home Nursing and Child Care

601 Help take care of a small child on 8 different occasions.*
602 Make a toy or play materials for a young child.
603 List equipment needed for a baby's bath, and show how to check for proper water temperature.
604 Learn the home care of virus, colds, flu, or a childhood disease when one of these appears in your home.
605 Demonstrate how to make up a bed for a patient, and how to arrange for a patient's comfort and convenience in bed.
606 Provide entertainment for a part of each day for a child who is confined to his room. Do this on 7 different occasions with approval of the child's mother.
607 Help take care of someone who is sick in your home, for 1 week. Avoid contagion.
608 Know how to clean a thermometer, how to read it, and how to shake it down.
609 Learn 10 kinds of liquids which may be used in an illness. Try to include the Basic Four foods.
610 Construct a bag with many pockets, to hang on a patient's bed to hold tissue, glasses, magazines, etc. Or prepare some other article or food for someone who is sick.

Safety and First Aid

701 Talk in your group about ways which you can keep yourself healthy, clean, and pretty. Carry out 2 ways which are especially hard for you, for 1 month.
702 Discuss in your group ways in which girls grow up. Invite a nurse, teacher, or other "specialist" to help answer questions you have on a topic such as menstruation.
703 Discuss with someone in your community whose job is health or safety, what he considers important for girls to know about health and safety. This might be a traffic policeman, a fireman, a doctor.

704 Prepare a chart with the phone numbers of the doctor, fire department, police department, poison center, clergyman, and other important and emergency numbers. Post near your telephone at home.

705 Make a list of all the dangerous objects and poisonous medicines found in your home. Decide whether they are kept in the safest possible place.

706 Learn the common causes of accidents in the following places: stairways, steps and halls, kitchen, porch, bedroom, and bathroom. Name ways that you can prevent accidents in your home.

707 Talk over with your family ways to prevent the spread of germs in your household.

708 Find out what your family should do if fire breaks out in your home. Talk this over with all the members of your family.

709 Help in a house and yard cleanup to eliminate fire hazards.

710 Name 3 common household insect pests and describe a method for controlling each.

711 Talk with your family about what safety measures are important in using electric appliances and what defects may cause accidents or fire.

712 In any car which has seatbelts, use them for 1 month each time you ride.

713 Check your family Christmas plans for safety precautions.

714 Demonstrate how you would call a doctor in case of illness or accident in the home, and what information you would give him.

715 Learn how to take care of 3 minor injuries such as splinters, bruises and bumps, and small cuts.

716 Invite a Red Cross First Aid Instructor to visit your group to demonstrate and discuss first aid honors.

717 Learn the 5 general directions for what to do at the scene of an accident.

718 Learn what to do if poisons are taken internally.

719 Find out if there is a Poison Control Center in your area. If so, learn the telephone number and put it by the telephone where it can be seen easily.

720 Learn the 2 pressure points in the arms or legs to control severe bleeding.

721 Learn well and demonstrate 1 of the 3 methods of artificial res-

piration: Oral (mouth-to-mouth); chest pressure-arm lift; or back pressure-arm lift.

722 Demonstrate how to prevent fainting and what to do for a person who has fainted.

723 Demonstrate to your group the method of lifting a heavy object so as not to hurt your back.

724 Learn and demonstrate the uses of the triangular bandage in emergencies.

725 Learn and demonstrate modern methods of caring for a burn.

726 Know proper first aid treatment for abrasions, floor burns, turned ankles, splinters.

727 Demonstrate the correct way of handling 2 types of wounds to prevent infection.

728 Equip your own First Aid Kit.

729 Tell when and how you would call the fire and police departments and any other emergency center.

730 Learn the two leading causes of fires and how to prevent them.

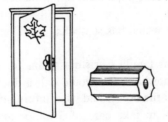

Outdoors Craft

Making New Friends in the World of Nature

101 With a cord 2 yards long, encircle a "claim" and list all the nature treasures you find in that spot.

102 Watch a sunrise, a sunset, or a storm gathering. Picture your reaction in words or a drawing.

103 Take a hike with several friends to collect nature items for use in a creative arts project. Carry out the project.

104 Find out what natural resources are in your immediate locality. Visit one of the areas, such as: stone quarry, mine, waterfall, lumber camp, etc., to learn more about the use of the natural resource.

105 Visit a dam. Find out why it was placed there and its usefulness for conservation, power, and recreation. Learn the size of the area influenced by this dam.

106 Find a fossil. Explain what a fossil is, and what yours indicates about the geological history of your locality.

107 Name at least 7 animals and explain the different ways in which they helped the early settlers.

108 Put up a light, and watch the creatures that come to it, or put up a salt lick and watch the animals that come to it.

109 Tell how birds, mammals, reptiles or amphibians protect themselves from their enemies. Do this from your own observations.

110 Find out from a local sportsman about well-known game in your locality. Report your most interesting findings to the group.

111 Listen to the sounds, follow the tracks, and learn the food habits of 2 different animals. Do this with a friend.

112 Learn about animals whose texture, form, or color serve as camouflage. Observe how this works with at least 2 different animals, and report this to your group.

113. Locate 4 homes of animals. Do this with a friend. In each case, notice the location, materials used, and who lives in the home. Find out why it is located this way, how the animals use the materials, and the suitability of the home to the animal.

114 Track an animal a quarter of a mile by its marks in the snow, sand, etc. Identify the animal by its tracks.

115 Know about and describe 5 snakes in your locality, including those which are poisonous.

116 Visit a fish hatchery, and find out what your state and the federal government do to protect and increase fish in your state.

117 Become a member of a Junior Audubon Program for at least 1 year. Do this with your group. Make use of the material that comes to you as a member.

118 Learn the size, colors, shape, and other characteristics of 2 different birds. Do this from personal observation.

119 Find 5 birds out of doors and observe them carefully enough so that you can describe them and recognize them when you see them again. Additional Honor: 5 birds in winter.

120 List all the different birds you see for a month. Record the date and place of each new entry.*

121 Watch where birds find their food; name and describe 2 birds which get their food from the air, and 2 from trees or other plants. Tell what they eat.

122 Watch birds build a nest. Tell what kind they built, what material was used, and the length of time they worked on it.

123 Hunt for birds' nests and tell where you saw 3 of them. Name and describe the birds using them. Do not disturb the birds or nests.

124 Be able to recognize and identify 5 birds by their call. Imitate 1 or more if possible.

125 Watch for the arrival or departure of 5 migrating birds, keeping a record of the dates when you saw them come or go. Find out where they spend winter and summer.

126 Draw and label at least 6 types of bird beaks. Tell how a bird with each type of beak is suited to procure its food.

127 Observe and identify 1 species each, of hawks and owls. Tell how hawks and owls are helpful to man.

128 Force into premature bloom at least 3 sprays of flowering shrubs or trees by bringing them into the house (forsythia, pussy willow, fruit tree sprigs, maple, etc.). Make an attractive arrangement.

129 Find 8 kinds of spring, summer, fall, or winter wild flowers in their natural surroundings. Describe them to your guardian or nature counselor and name them correctly, telling where you saw them.

130 Plant and care for a window garden from kitchen cuttings. Use such fruits and vegetables as the carrot, beet, radish, yam, pineapple, and avocado.

131 Identify 5 plants by their odor, and tell something about each one. Additional Honor: identify by feel.

132 Find and point out to your guardian or nature counselor 3 kinds of plants injurious to people or cattle.

133 Distinguish (without touching) between poison ivy and Virginia creeper (by mistake called woodbine), or between poison sumac and harmless sumac, or be able to identify poison oak. Explain what is the protection against each, and the follow-up treatment.

134 Find 5 native plants which were used for food, clothes, or other

purposes, by the Indians. Tell how these plants were prepared for use.

135 Find and name 5 plants that grow in sand, or in swamps, or in the shade, or in the sun.

136 Find 4 different kinds of ferns growing in their natural surroundings, and be able to name them.

137 Find 2 kinds of ferns that are in fruit and tell how they reproduce.

138 Plant a fern garden, or fill a fern basket, using 4 different kinds of ferns. Make labels to identify them.

139 Make drawings, photographs, or cut-out silhouettes, showing the contour of 10 trees.

140 Lay a trail for ½ mile or more. Do this with 2 or more friends. Have 2 or more different people follow it.

141 Follow a trail (with 2 or more friends) which has been laid by others than yourself.

142 Draw a map of your own or a friend's yard. Picture on it the location of all trees, plants, flowers and shrubs. Name each.

143 Use a compass to find your way to a point 1 mile distant.

144 Use a map to locate a trail, and follow it for at least 1 mile. Do this with an adult.

145 Make a map, with your group, of your city neighborhood. Show the location, the names and information about plants and other interesting natural features (hill, river, etc.) of the neighborhood. Share this "City Nature Trail" with another group, or with newcomers to the neighborhood.

146 Make a dip net for collecting fresh-water insects.

147 Make a scrapbook about your favorite nature subject. Illustrate with clippings, your own sketches, photographs, or mounted specimens.

148 Start a collection with 20 poems about your favorite nature subjects. Note author and source.

149 Make a plaster of Paris plaque of a bird track you have found.

150 Make a plaster of Paris plaque of a mammal footprint.

Note: Additional honors about making new friends in the world of nature are found in Science Craft.

Conservation

201 Visit a U.S. Forest Station. Find out what the Forest Ranger

does and how you can help him.

202 Clean up some area or street which thoughtless people have left littered.

203 Find out about 2 organizations that work to protect wildlife.

204 Name your state flower, tree, and bird. Give a summary of your state conservation laws as they apply to plants and birds.

205 Learn about an animal or bird now in danger of becoming extinct. Tell why there is the danger, what measures are being taken to protect this creature, and why we should protect it.

206 Learn about an animal or bird that has become extinct within the last 50 years, and tell why it became extinct.

207 Learn the Conservation Pledge, and tell how you are keeping it.

208 Do 1 project from the Camp Fire Girls *Conservation* book, alone or with your group.

209 Find out what the Conservation Committee in your community is doing to aid local conservation and how your group can help.

210 Tell the part trees and forests play in conservation of wild life, soil, and water supply. Illustrate with observations and facts about your part of the country.

211 Celebrate Arbor Day by planting a tree or a shrub. Plan a ceremony for this occasion.

212 Plant 2 trees where needed, at least 1 foot high.

213 Plant a cover crop (grass, clover, sweet clover, wild rose, etc.) on the sides of a new highway cut. Do this with the consent and support of your local highway commission.

214 Make a tree, forest, wild flower, or bird conservation poster, 12 x 15 inches or larger, which is to be used in a display.

215 Have a wild flower conservation exhibit to show which flowers may be picked and which should not be. Pictures, photographs or slides could be used to show the rare flowers.

216 Make a suet feeder and keep a record for 1 month of the birds that use it.

217 Place your discarded Christmas tree outdoors, and change it into one which the birds will enjoy.

218 Make and maintain a bird bath that birds use. Keep a list for 1 month of the birds that you see use it.

Making Things from Natural Materials

301 Arrange a seasonal bouquet (spring, summer, autumn or winter) of wild flowers, grasses, leaves, or seeds.

302 Make an article from clay found in your locality.

303 Make jewelry from sea shells you have found.

304 Weave a mat of cane, reed, rushes, or other wild material.

305 Make a letter opener or a knife, fork or spoon, out of material found out of doors.

306 Make an Indian loom and weave a rug on it, using rushes, grass, or other outdoor material.

307 Make a strong basket of wildwood material which will hold at least 1 quart of grain or berries.

Fire Building and Outdoor Cooking

Note: These activities should be done with skilled adults present and with safety rules in mind.

401 Learn and demonstrate proper care and use of a knife, including sharpening.

402 Learn and demonstrate the care and use of hand axe.

403 Learn and demonstrate the use and care of a saw.

404 Sharpen a hand axe, using a file or whetstone.

405 Know the reasons for fire regulations and precautions in the area in which you are hiking, cooking out, or camping.

406 Demonstrate proper care and use of matches on hiking and camping trips.

407 Waterproof matches for a cookout or a camping trip. Pack them properly for carrying.

408 Collect and arrange a woodpile for use in fire building. Sort the wood into piles of tinder, kindling, and fuel.

409 Demonstrate the proper fire safety measures for laying and extinguishing outdoor fires.

410 Select, name and use 3 kinds of wood for a quick blaze. Explain when it is desirable to cook over a quick blaze.

411 Select, name, and use 3 kinds of wood for coals. Explain when it is preferable to cook over a bed of coals.

412 Lay a cooking fire and keep it going while a meal is cooked.

413 Build and use a crisscross fire.

414 Build and use a hunter's and trapper's fire.

415 Construct a reflector oven and bake biscuits or some other appetizing dish.

416 Demonstrate proper safety measures for laying, lighting, using, and extinguishing a charcoal fire. Use a charcoal fire to cook 1 dish.

417 Make an exhibit of 3 kinds of fires.

418 Make and use 3 fuzz sticks.

419 Make a fireplace brush or broom from the wood of the yellow birch.

420 Build a council fire and keep it burning during the ceremony. Do this with a partner.

421 Prepare and pack a trailside lunch for 2 or more people.

422 Help to collect and pack food for a group outing.

423 Cook part of an outdoor meal on a gypsy (tin can) stove. Do this with a friend.

424 Assist with cooking and serving a one-pot meal.

425 Cook a bread twist on a stick.

426 Cook biscuits or a dessert in foil.

427 Roast 6 ears of corn over coals.

428 Bake or steam fish or sea food out of doors.

429 Cook a meal without using utensils.

430 Cook a meal in foil: potato, meat, and vegetables. Be responsible for preparing food, wrapping the foil, and timing.

431 Cook potatoes 3 different ways out of doors.

432 Cook 2 recipes in a Dutch oven out of doors.

433 Originate and successfully try out an outdoor cooking recipe.

434 Help with cooking 2 or more meals outdoors.

435 Prepare and cook, with 3 others, 1 outdoor meal for 4 or more persons. Plan a balanced menu. Write it out, and list quantities and prices. Gather wood and make the fire. Clean up afterwards.

436 Clean up camp garbage and refuse after 3 meals. Dispose of it by burning or burying, or with the proper use of trash cans.

437 Make a tin can gypsy stove and use it.

438 Make from tin cans, and use, 2 pieces of camping equipment.

439 Make a knapsack or 2 bags or cases for carrying camp supplies.

440 Make a cheesecloth dish-sterilizing bag to be used for your own dishes on a camping trip. Use for at least 3 meals.

Knots and Lashing

501 Collect samples of different kinds of rope or cord, and explain suitable use of each.

502 Learn and demonstrate the slip knot and square knot, and know their uses.

503 Make an article such as a dog leash or bag handles, using square knots.

504 Learn and use a simple hitch, half hitch, and 2 half hitches. Know when to use them.

505 Learn and demonstrate the use of clove hitch.

506 Learn and demonstrate use of bowline knot.

507 Use a sheet bend to tie 2 rope ends together.

508 Make a piece of camping equipment (or a gadget) using square lashing. Earn extra honors by doing the same thing with diagonal lashing, sheer lashing, and continuous lashing.

509 Whip the ends of rope to prevent fraying.

510 Make a chart showing at least 10 different kinds of knots. Label each with name and uses.

Hiking and Camping Out

Note: Responsible adults (number set by Camp Fire Girls standards) must accompany you on hikes and camping trips.

601 Make a "sit-upon" with a waterproof covering; use on a hike or camping trip.

602 Make a ditty bag for use on camping trips. Use rope handles passing through grommets.

603 Make a hike kit or pack, and use on a hike.

604 Take part in a "campers' fashion show" to demonstrate the proper clothing and equipment for a hike.

605 Demonstrate or tell your group at least 5 rules for good outdoor behavior in using private or public-owned property.

606 Decide with your group on at least 5 important Hiker's and Camper's Rules for Safety and Courtesy. Help to make a poster or exhibit or give a talk to explain them.

607 Make an envelope or flipflop bedding roll and tie it.

608 Pack, roll, and tie a sleeping bag.

609 Take a rain or snow hike with your group, being sure you are properly dressed.

610 Go on a hike of 1 mile or more with your group. Take your lunch.

611 Help to plan, and then go on a hike of 2 miles or more, taking your lunch along.

612 Participate in a back yard sleep-out.

613 Make a personal equipment list before you start on a camping trip. Check it before returning.

614 Plan and go on a camp overnight, eating supper and breakfast, cooking 1 or both meals out of doors.

615 Go on a camping trip with your family or your group, sleeping in a tent at least 2 consecutive nights.

616 Use a knapsack cache while on a camping trip or hike.

617 Learn and demonstrate how to select a good spot to place your sleeping bag or bed roll for sleeping on the ground.

618 Make a bed on the ground and sleep on it over night.

619 Set up a poncho shelter.

620 Make a sleeping hammock, using canvas or blanket, and sleep on it for 5 nights.

621 Select a location and erect a tent, with a partner.

622 Take down tent with a partner, and fold it properly.

623 Demonstrate that you know the proper handling of tent ropes during and after a rain.

624 Know about first aid for scratches and cuts, bites of insects, chiggers and ticks.

625 Tell how to prevent a blister and how to care for one.

626 Discuss how to prevent sunburn. Tell about emergency treatment for it and for other burns.

627 Help to make a group First Aid Kit for hikes or overnight.

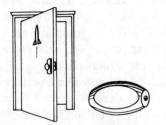

Science Craft (former title, Frontiers)

Note: All collecting should be done with due regard for good conservation practices. All experiments should be carried out with due regard for safety practices.

Science Research and Resources

101 Take a trip to see a sunrise, a waterfall, an unusual garden, a zoo, or a bird sanctuary. Go with your parents or group.

102 Visit a museum of science or a children's museum. Tell your group about your experiences.

103 Make up and act out a play, charades, skit, or pantomime about a famous scientist.

104 Set up a laboratory where you may experiment with a subject of your interest.

105 Choose a science experiment you would like to perform. Have it approved by your guardian or your science teacher. Demonstrate and explain it to a group.

106 Help your group have a science party with decorations and games planned around the Science Craft. Come dressed to impersonate a famous scientist. Put on a charade to act out one of his or her achievements.

107 Have a group science show at which experiments are performed, and exhibits, projects and hobbies are displayed.

108 Participate in a community science show or science fair.

109 Participate in a national or international science fair. If you receive recognition, report this to Camp Fire Girls, Inc.

Terra Firma

201 Take a trip to the florist and identify 5 plants that are new to you.

202 Care for 2 indoor plants for a season.

203 Plant at least 3 seeds you find in your kitchen and report what happens.

204 Plant grass seed on a damp sponge or layer of wet cotton. Keep it damp. Keep a record of what happens.

205 Grow a plant from the pit of an avocado or other fruit.

206 Grow 1 kind of seed in each: water, sand, and soil. Compare the rate of growth and watch the results.

207 Discover how seeds differ. Plant 3 different kinds and watch the plants develop. Tell about the rate of growth and about other observations you make.

208 Collect 10 kinds of seeds. Mount and label them. Include seeds that fly, float, are shot and are carried, and identify them.

209 Discover what plants will grow new plants from cuttings. Do this by putting 5 different stems with leaves in water or moist soil.

210 Root a vine cutting, such as ivy, philodendron, etc., in water. Then pot it and have it take root. Care for it for a season.

211 Start a tree or shrub from a cutting, or graft or bud a tree or shrub.

212 Discover by experimenting which of 6 plants will root from leaves.

213 Grow a plant from a root. Use water or moist sand. This might be a sweet potato or carrot. Care for it for a season

214 Grow 3 different plants from bulbs in the spring. Dig them up in the fall and record your observations of the roots.

215 Make a chart showing the parts of a flower. This may be drawn or have actual parts pasted on.

216 Select 1 plant or flower growing out of doors. Record the changes in its size, color, and shape during 1 month.

217 Tell the age and life story of a tree, as revealed in its rings. Illustrate with either the actual stump or cross section, or a photograph or a drawing of it.

218 Keep a diary of a tree for 1 season, illustrating it with sketches or snapshots. Give dates of leaves, blossoms, fruits, bird arrivals, etc.

219 Learn 5 ways for growing new plants. Use 3 ways to grow new plants.

220 Observe 4 plants which divide themselves into new plants.

221 Cross-pollinate any 1 kind of plant ana grow a plant from the seeds of such pollination.

222 Construct a hothouse for plants, using a clear plastic material.

223 Collect and press 10 wild flowers, ferns, or tree leaves. Label each with name, date, and place found.

224 Collect, mount, and label 5 kinds of grasses.

225 Mount and label twigs from 10 kinds of trees or shrubs. Or mount and label the winter buds of 10 trees or shrubs of different kinds, the cones of 10 kinds of coniferous trees, or pods or seeds of 10 deciduous trees or shrubs.

226 Make prints of 10 wild flowers, ferns, leaves, or grasses. This may be a combination. Label each with name, place, and date found.

227 Make and maintain a miniature or dish garden, from plants you have collected. Identify each plant.

228 Plant and maintain a terrarium with ferns, mosses, small plants, etc. Identify each plant you have collected.

229 Maintain a desert terrarium, using plants you have collected

from dry, sandy soil. Identify each plant.

230 Plant a terrarium with at least 3 different types of fungi. Keep it out of direct light, water often; observe the growth.

231 Place pieces of moldy bread in 4 separate, covered jars. Put one in warm dark cupboard, one in refrigerator, one in sunlight, and one in cupboard without cover. Compare growth of mold after several days.

232 Tie a clear plastic bag over leaves and stem of plant. Set the plant in the sun for several hours. Observe what happens on the inside of the bag.

233 Plant 3 identical seeds in each of 2 containers. Place one container in a sunny location, the other in a shady spot. Observe the rate of growth and appearance of each.

234 Plant 3 seeds in each of 2 containers. Place one container in a warm location, the other in a cool spot. Observe the rate of growth and appearance of each.

235 Plant 3 identical seeds in each of 2 containers. Water one container frequently, the other only occasionally. Observe the rate of growth and appearance of each.

236 Demonstrate to a group the difference in absorption of water where earth is covered with vegetation and where it is bare.

237 Talk with a geologist about the formation of the earth's surface and its composition in your community.

238 Collect samples of sand, silt, clay, loam. Find out how they differ.

239 Study 1 square yard of soil. Dig into the soil. Identify the different layers and insect life you find.

240 Collect 3 rocks. Label each and tell how each was formed.

241 Collect 4 kinds of rock which occur naturally in your locality. Identify and label each.

242 Put your own rock and mineral collection in a small box. Number each specimen and paste the key (answers) on the cover of the box. Try exchanging specimens.

243 Learn how coal is formed and talk about this with a younger person. Show specimens if possible.

244 Explain how mineral crystals differ in shape. Demonstrate with a crystal garden you have made with coal.

245 Make 2 illustrated charts: one which shows foods that supply minerals to your body and one which shows minerals that we wear. Label the illustrations.

Animal Life

301 Learn which animals are found in your locale. Find out about their food, shelter and means of protection. Be able to identify as many as you can.

302 Identify 3 different classes of animals and learn why each is suited to its particular environment.

303 Name at least 6 animals of a class. Tell on which continent they are to be found, and several interesting facts about each.

304 Select 10 animals. Find out the name for their young and what they are called as a class.

305 Describe the many ways different animals protect themselves.

306 Learn 4 different ways that animals use their tails. Observe as many as possible.

307 Observe what happens during the birth of an animal.

308 Observe and record the family life of hamsters or guinea pigs, for 3 months.

309 Learn to identify 4 kinds of mammals which are found in another part of the country, through visiting a zoo, a museum, or seeing a movie.

310 Learn about 2 animals that are now extinct and tell why it is thought they became extinct.

311 Learn which birds are found in your locale. Find out their migratory, nesting, and feeding habits.

312 Watch the nest of a mother bird. Record what happens before hatching and afterwards until the baby birds leave their nest.

313 Hatch eggs in an incubator. Sketch or photograph the stages during the hatchery period.

314 Start a feather collection with at least 10 feathers. Try to find the species of bird each came from and what purpose the feather served. Examine the feathers under a magnifying glass.

315 Watch a spider spin her web, and tell how this is done.

316 Identify and raise a caterpillar; care for chrysalis or cocoon until it comes out as butterfly or moth.

317 Collect some cocoons and keep them; dampen them occasionally until they hatch.

318 Tell in what ways 5 insects are helpful to man. Be able to recognize them from personal observation.

319 Tell from personal observation how 2 insects make their noises. Show specimens.

320 Observe insects at night by placing a lighted blue bulb outdoors

on top of a sheet. Watch the insects come and identify at least 5 different kinds.

321 Collect insect eggs and keep them until they hatch.

322 Collect 8 insects of different orders. Label each with name, date, and place found.

323 Observe an ant colony, for an hour. Notice the activity of the ants, and anything else you can find out about them.

324 Learn about the life and different jobs of ants in an ant colony. Do this from personal observation and from study. Tell your group.

325 Make an ant house; keep an ant colony, and observe their habits.

326 Compare the lives of the ant and bee. Be able to tell of similarities when you report to a group.

327 Learn about the life and different jobs of bees in a bee colony. Do this from personal observation and from study. Tell your group.

328 Observe a crab and keep a diary for 1 hour of what it does.

329 Observe a snail or slug and watch its movements. Feed it lettuce and watch it eat.

330 Find and keep a pet turtle, giving it proper food and care for 1 month. Tell what kind it is. See if you can find 1 other kind of turtle native to your state. If possible, observe a turtle laying her eggs and tell your family or Camp Fire group about it.

Atmosphere

401 Visit a United States Weather Station. Before you go, think of questions you would like to ask.

402 Play a circle game in which each person tells how weather made a difference in her life during one month.

403 Explain what causes rain to fall, everything that might happen to it on the earth's surface, and how it returns to the atmosphere again.

404 Tell about the various types of clouds and what they signify. Make a chart to show their differences.

405 Describe several types of storms, giving their major characteristic.

406 Examine snow crystals under a microscope or hand lens. Draw sketches of several.

407 Describe and explain the formation of rainbows, rings around the moon, and the colors of a sunset.

408 Build a simple sundial and explain how you tell time by it.

409 Make a chemical hygrometer which indicates by its color whether the atmosphere is damp or dry.

410 Become familiar with the weather page in your newspaper and keep a record of the temperature in 5 different sections of the country for a week. Point out the changes and differences to your group.

411 Know how 4 or 5 instruments are used by weathermen in predicting the weather.

412 Make at least one weather instrument and check your findings for a week with those printed in the newspaper or broadcast via TV, radio or telephone.

413 Make a weather station in your back yard with a rain gauge and thermometer. Record the daily precipitation and temperature and the weather for a month.

414 Demonstrate how sound is made, using a vibrating object.

415 Experiment with 3 musical instruments to learn how music is made by air vibration.

416 Make a simple musical instrument using materials found out of doors (reeds, bark, leaves, stems, shells). Play upon it.

417 Find out how air enables airplanes to take off and remain aloft.

418 Perform an experiment to show how temperature affects air pressure.

419 Learn several ways air works for us. Perform an experiment to illustrate one of these.

420 Learn about the causes of air pollution in your community.

421 Learn the names of the 4 layers of the atmosphere and the depth and characteristics of each.

Water

501 Use water in its 3 forms.

502 Visit the water reservoir which serves your community. Learn the steps taken to prepare the water for household use.

503 Tell your group the percentage of the human body that is water, and its various functions for the body.

504 Observe high and low tides and record the time for 3 consecutive days. Tell your group why the times differ.

505 Explain what causes tides, and how they affect human activity.

506 Find out where the ocean currents run, and how they affect land temperature and sea life.

507 Perform an experiment to desalinate water.

508 Learn how submarines submerge.

509 Demonstrate that salt water has a greater density than fresh water.

510 Perform an experiment to prove that an empty ship rides higher than one with cargo.

511 Learn about some oceanography explorations being carried on at this time.

512 Find out all you can about minerals in the sea and how scientists are working to make them available and useful to man.

513 Make a picture map to show some of the natural resources that are found in the ocean.

514 Find and identify 4 kinds of water plants.

515 Tell about the 3 color groups of seaweeds, using a chart you have made with mounted specimens.

516 Collect 5 kinds of seaweeds. Mount them on heavy paper and label with name and where found.

517 Collect with a dip net or strainer, 3 forms of fresh-water life; identify each (insect, snail, leech, crustacean, etc.). Keep in shallow white pan for 1 day and report what happens.

518 Sketch and record the development of frogs' eggs until they become frogs. Do this from your own observations.

519 Identify 3 live fish found in a brook, lake, or ocean and learn about their food habits. Tell your group.

520 Report to others how fish live naturally in water. Compare this with the way boats are made, and the way human beings try to adjust to movement in water.

521 Give a report on the life story of the salmon, using illustrations. Provide tasty salmon tidbits for your audience.

522 Maintain a balanced aquarium for at least 1 month, having 3 kinds of water plants in a fine gravel and 3 kinds of goldfish or tropical fish.

523 Start or add to your collection of seashells. Mount and identify 10 specimens, including place and date found.

Outer Space

601 Visit a planetarium and learn how the telescope is used.

602 Interview a scientist and report to your group about the experiments in which he is engaged.

603 Know the difference between a star and a planet. Point out 2 examples of each in the sky.

604 Tell a group about the planets in our solar system.

605 Chart the North Star and the Big and Little Dippers from your sky observations at 3 hour intervals in one night. Explain their change of positions.

606 Locate some of the summer and winter constellations with a planisphere.

607 Draw 5 constellations and be able to locate them in the sky.

608 Point out and name 7 constellations. Tell an interesting fact about each.

609 Point out and name 7 stars; name the constellation in which they appear. Tell an interesting fact about each.

610 Make an umbrella planetarium. Explain it to a younger group of children.

611 Observe a meteor shower in mid-August, October, January, or December. Report to your group.

612 Observe the eight phases of the moon. Note the varying shapes of the moon and its location in the sky.

613 Perform an experiment for your group with a flashlight and a ball, which shows the phases of the moon.

614 Perform an experiment to show what happens during an eclipse.

615 Perform an experiment with your group to show how the earth moving around the sun brings about the days, the seasons, and the year.

616 Chart the revolution of the earth on its axis, as it moves around the sun at different seasons of the year.

617 Visit a space center or launching site.

618 Watch a man-made satellite in the sky. Report the location where it first appears and the direction in which it disappears. Tell in what ways that satellite is an aid to science.

619 Record the history of a single space effort from the time it is first announced until it is successful or scrapped. Illustrate with newspaper clippings and pictures.

620 Compare the airplane used by the Wright brothers with a present day space capsule. Tell your group some of the differences.

621 Start or add to your book on outer space. Use illustrations, dates of important happenings, clippings, etc.

622 Give or write a brief biographical sketch of a favorite American astronaut.

623 Learn about the qualifications and training of the American astronauts.

624 Make an exhibit of illustrations of the different kinds of satellites launched by the United States, such as weather, manned, communication, etc.

625 Find out interesting facts about American manned orbital flights and tell your group about 2 or 3. Include pictures and clippings if you wish.

626 Find out about the major contributions which the United States and other countries have made to space exploration.

627 Discuss or show how exploration of space benefits mankind.

628 Help your group have a space party with favors, games, hats, or some other part of costume related to space.

629 Make up and act out a story about space exploration. Include space clothing, food, communications in space. Do this with others.

630 Use your imagination in writing a story about space exploration in the future. Read it to your group.

631 Tell the legends of 5 constellations to a group of 5 or more persons. Point them out in the sky, on a chart or drawing, or on a diagram.

632 Learn about your own sign of the zodiac. Have a zodiac birthday party with your group at which each tells about her sign.

Communications

701 Visit an amateur radio station or ham radio operator. Find out about the broadcast frequency and the ham operator's log.

702 Visit a radio or a TV station. Have an engineer explain the operations, wave lengths, etc.

703 Go on a conducted tour of a telegraph office.

704 Visit a museum (the historical or archeological rooms) or an industrial showroom. See how many instruments you can find that have been or are used for communication.

705 Report to your group on the method of mass communication today and compare with the methods of communications used centuries ago.

706 Collect stories on the usefulness of radio, TV, or of radar and sonar.

707 Prepare and give a mock radio broadcast, with homemade mechanical sound effects.

708 Make a string telephone that will conduct messages around corners as well as in a straight line. Use it to talk to someone.

709 Make a telephone with which you can actually talk to a person at a distance. Tell how this is similar to and different from, a real telephone.

710 Perform an experiment to show how sound travels.

711 Set up and print an invitation, a program, or a newspaper on a hand printing press.

712 Make a hectograph and produce at least 15 usable copies of an announcement, program, menu, etc.

713 Send a message to a friend, using heliograph signals.

714 Make a Morse code sending key (either sound or light) and receiver. Send and receive 2 messages.

715 Participate in an exhibit of instruments of communication. Identify each entry and give information on each as to how used.

Transportation

801 Travel by plane, train, or boat. Observe all you can about the vehicle's construction and operation. Give a report or write a log of your trip.

802 Go on a group trip to visit a railroad yard or roundhouse. Inspect the engines.

803 Take a trip with your Camp Fire group on a streamliner train. Before the trip talk about things to look for; observe facilities for comfort such as air conditioning, lighting, seats, speed, and smoothness of travel. Share observations afterward.

804 Go on a group excursion to a dock or freight wharf. Explore the interior of a cargo or passenger vessel if possible.

805 Visit a plant or factory which assembles or makes planes, cars, trucks, railroad cars, etc. Do this with your group.

806 Identify the major types of land transportation. Know their special features and uses.

807 Identify 10 different types of boats. Know their particular uses and characteristics.

808 Identify the major types of aircraft. Know their special features and uses.

809 Help prepare a show, exhibit, or demonstration, to tell the story of travel by land, water, or air from early times to the present.

810 Tell some legends or stories about early attempts to fly, or about

early railroad engines, early automobiles, or the first power ships or submarines.

811 Make a model of a plane, ship, or train.

812 Identify 4 different boats which are unique to one particular continent. Tell why and how they are used.

813 Help present a skit or program to show ways in which communication and transportation depend on each other.

814 Read about, and observe how transportation is affected by weather. Give 10 examples.

815 Chart a real or imaginary trip by referring to an air map, a road map, or a nautical map.

816 Play 3 games in which a compass is used.

817 Learn how to measure distance by pace and make a simple map, using a compass.

818 Learn how to "box" a compass.

819 Make a floating needle compass.

820 Play compass games to help others learn how to use a compass.

Energy

901 Visit a local electric generating plant.

902 Visit a private or government power dam, or collect pictures and information on power dams. Exhibit your information and materials.

903 Visit a private generating system on a farm. Describe your experiences to your group.

904 Visit the air conditioning plant in a building. Explain the difference between a heating plant and an air conditioning plant.

905 Examine 3 electric light bulbs of different size. Notice the wattage of each, and where each would be best used.

906 Learn about direct and alternating currents, their uses and differences. Perform an experiment using direct or alternating current.

907 Find out about the source of atomic energy and the useful ways in which atomic energy is used.

908 Find out about the major sources and uses of energy. Give examples when you report to a group about this.

909 Perform experiments showing how light rays are reflected through glass, water, and air.

910 Demonstrate how light rays may be bent.

911 Conduct an experiment to show that light and sound travel at different speeds.

912 Make a model water wheel to show how it operates.

913 Perform experiments showing the following: what magnets attract, why magnets are stronger at their poles.

914 Demonstrate by pantomime the 4 major uses of magnets.

Chemistry

1001 Write an invitation to a party or a letter using invisible ink.

1002 Place a cup of sugar, a piece of rock salt, and a piece of hard candy in 3 separate glasses of water. Do not stir. Describe what happens to each material after 2 days.

1003 Dissolve sugar and salt in different containers of water. Let water evaporate. Describe crystals formed.

1004 Find a piece of limestone; drop some lemon juice on it. Describe what happens and explain it.

1005 Watch atoms split by using a clock with a luminous dial and a magnifying glass. Talk about what you see.

1006 Prove in an experiment that air exerts pressure.

1007 Prove in an experiment that heat affects air pressure.

1008 Show in an experiment that a fire can't burn without oxygen.

1009 Observe 4 different kinds of oxidation. Describe what you see.

1010 Learn ways oxygen is used. Perform an experiment to demonstrate 1 of these.

1011 Learn several uses of carbon dioxide. Perform an experiment to demonstrate one.

1012 Put on a chemical magic show with your group.

Photography

1101 Demonstrate how to load a camera, to focus, to judge distance, and to take a picture.

1102 Go on a camera hike. Take at least 2 good pictures.

1103 Take 3 successful time exposure pictures.

1104 Start a photo album in which you keep pictures you have taken.

1105 Take part in a group photography exhibit. Show pictures you have taken.

1106 Classify and index a collection of slides for your family.

1107 Learn how to operate and care for a slide projector. Show at least 20 slides to your own or another group. Explain the story behind the slides.

1108 Visit a photography shop or pnotographer's darkroom with your group to learn how pictures are developed.

1109 Learn to develop your own pictures. Develop 5.

1110 Make a camera using a cigar box, a cork, and metal foil. Take 1 picture.

Sports and Games Craft

Games for Fun and Skill

101 Learn a skill that you do not know, such as jumping rope, rope-spinning, hop scotch, skating, jacks, marbles.

102 Learn 3 new jumping rope rhymes and jump to them.

103 Learn 3 active group games that are new to you, such as hide and seek, run sheep run, prisoner's base. Play these with a group.

104 Take part several times in at least 3 kinds of relay races which are new to you. These may be either circle or line relays.

105 Learn to play, and demonstrate a fair degree of skill, in 1 of the following team games: circle kickball, volleyball, softball, basketball, dodgeball, field hockey.

106 Play 3 games new to you, which are played by children of other countries.

107 Learn to play well 3 games which might be played with a handicapped person.

108 Be responsible for teaching or leading the games played at 3 group meetings.

109 Take part in a play day.

110 Play any of the following for at least 8 hours: serial darts, deck

tennis, paddle tennis, table tennis, shuffleboard, golf, tether ball, punch ball, horse shoes, croquet.

111 Teach someone else, younger than you, 1 of the games mentioned in honor #110.

112 Be responsible for setting up game equipment 6 times.

113 Learn the rules and scoring and play 1 game of the following: canasta, pinochle, monopoly, backgammon, gin rummy, chess, hearts.

114 Make up a game and play it with others.

Games to Make

201 Paint a table game, such as tick-tack-toe, on cardboard.

202 Make a hobbyhorse, using such equipment as a broom stick and a stuffed sock head, and give it to a child.

203 Make a set of beanbags for use in a game.

204 Make a beanbag target out of heavy cardboard or wood, and decorate it. Number the holes in the target for winning points.

205 Make and decorate a nest of at least 3 boxes or tin cans, for a pitching button game.

Keeping Fit

301 Do a series of fitness exercises such as those in the "Keeping Fit" chapter, for 10 minutes each day for 2 weeks.*

302 Run a city block or its equivalent, 5 times a week for 1 month.*

303 Do a high jump over a string or bamboo pole into a sandpile, with the string at 3 feet height.

304 Take part in physical fitness activities such as Tortoise and Hare, Wind in the Trees, Bunny Hop, Bear Walk, Leap Frog, Measuring Worm, or Wheelbarrow, for a total of at least 5 hours.

305 Walk a total distance of 15 miles. Do this within a 3-week period.

306 Walk 1 mile every day for 2 weeks.

Folk Games and Dances

401 Learn and play three singing games.

402 Learn to dance 3 circle dances.

403 Learn the basic square dance calls and terms. Show that you can perform the steps gracefully.

404 Learn 3 popular square dances.

405 Learn 3 folk dances of other countries.

406 Learn 3 American folk dances other than square dances.

407 Take part in a square dance party given by your group for your parents.

408 Take part in a performance of folk dances to which others are invited.

Sports for You

501 Learn and observe the 12 rules for safe riding of the Bicycle Institute of America.

502 Make and use a chart of safety check points to look for, to maintain a safe bicycle.

503 Participate in a bicycle safety project for your group, school, or community.

504 Go fishing with a group of not more than 6-8 persons, at least one of whom is an adult. Observe all safety rules.

505 Make a live bait container.

506 Learn to cast and reel in.

507 Catch and identify 3 different kinds of fish.

508 Learn rules and scoring for one of the following, well enough to play an actual game: tennis, deck tennis, badminton, table tennis, bowling, shuffleboard.

509 Perform 5 successful tennis serves in a row, 4 times in any 4 days.

510 Demonstrate the difference between a net shot and a baseline or back court stroke, in tennis.

511 Demonstrate a drop shot in your badminton game.

512 Serve 10 high-deep serves in badminton. Do this from your service line.

513 Serve 10 short net-skimming serves in badminton. Do this from your service line.

514 Know safety rules and precautions for archery—as they apply to your equipment, your audience, and yourself.

515 Know the parts of the bow and arrow and the scoring values of the different colored circles on the target.

516 Demonstrate the proper method of drawing arrows from target and scoring.

517 Demonstrate how to find the point of aim and tell why your aim changes as you move toward or away from the target.

518 Shoot 24 arrows (4 ends of 6 arrows) at 15 yards and make a score of at least 50 points.

519 Demonstrate good form in shooting, from the time you take your position until you have released your arrow.

520 Earn any of the ratings as recognized by the American Archery Association of the U.S.

521 Participate in an archery tournament.

522 Mount, ride a horse, using a walking gait, for at least 100 yards, and dismount.

523 Learn how to guide a horse around trees, and out of trouble spots along trail.

524 Demonstrate ability to post.

525 Demonstrate ability to canter.

526 Demonstrate ability to gallop.

527 Feed and water a horse at least twice.

528 Know the parts of a saddle and be able to distinguish between a Western and an English saddle.

529 Ride a horse 1 hour daily, in any 5 days. Explain why a good rider always walks his horse the first and last mile.*

530 Demonstrate how to approach, catch (in a corral or in a stall) lead, and tie a horse.

531 Participate in class events in a horse show.*

Swimming

All swimming honors have been checked with the American Red Cross.

601 Tell your group 10 safety rules for swimming and diving.

602 Put your face into water, and open your eyes enough to identify an object under water. Do this 10 times in 3 days. (This may be done in a basin of clear water.)

603 Do jellyfish float and hold for 5 seconds. Do this 5 times in 2 days.

604 Stoop down in water at least up to your waist, and pick up with your hands 5 different small objects from the bottom.

605 Do a prone float 5 times during a half hour period.

606 Face float 5 seconds, 6 times in 1 day.

607 Float 10 seconds on your back, 5 times in 1 day.

608 Swim 10 feet on face, using legs only.

609 Swim 10 feet on back, using legs only.

610 Tread water 1 minute.

611 Jump off a dock, board, or the side of a pool, feet first into water at least up to your waist. Do it 3 times in 1 day.

612 Jump into water at least up to your armpits and swim 25 feet.

613 Dive into the water and swim 50 feet.

614 Swim, float, or tread water, or do a combination of these for 10 minutes.

615 Change body position from back to front and to back again, while sculling 60 feet.

616 Swim 1 of the following strokes in good form: elementary back stroke, side stroke, crawl, racing back or breast stroke, for a distance of 60 feet.

617 Swim 40 yards.

618 Swim 40 yards, fully dressed: (shorts, blouse, sneakers).

619 Do any 2 of the following dives in good form: standing front, running front, swan, back, forward or backward somersault, or any other standard dive.

620 Demonstrate the rescue of a person without getting into the water yourself. Use some object between you and the victim such as a board, tire, inner tube, life jacket.

621 Take part in a water pageant or water play day.

622 Plan and have a Swimming Party. In the group discuss and agree upon adequate safety rules. Follow them. There must be a qualified water safety instructor in charge of the swimming.

Small Craft

701 Prepare a list of 15 small craft safety rules, for passengers and skippers. (Canoeing, boating, sailing, and for motor boats.)

702 With craft, demonstrate a working knowledge of the "Rules of the Road" that apply in your area.

703 Send and receive 3 messages, using the signal flag code.

704 Send and receive 3 messages, using the wigwag or the flash code.

705 Know and use at least 2 knots commonly used to secure a boat, and 2 splices used in boating.

706 Name the parts of 2 of the following craft and explain the maintenance of both: rowboat, canoe, sailboat.

707 Demonstrate proper method of launching, casting off, entering, beaching or docking, mooring or anchoring, 1 of the following: rowboat, canoe, sailboat.

In a rowboat:

708 Demonstrate rowing: 1) a straight course, 2) gradual turn, 3) sharp turn.

709 Show good form in rowing, back water stroke, and sculling.

710 Row 10 miles in any 5 days, or ½ hour a day for 5 days.

In a canoe:

711 Demonstrate proper form in paddling in a straight line, reverse paddling, and steering, as directed by instructor.

712 Demonstrate (with partner): 1) bow stroke, 2) back water stroke, 3) forward and reverse sweeps, 4) draw stroke and 5) "J" stroke.

713 Paddle for 300 yards, not lifting paddle from water.

714 Demonstrate changing paddling positions in a canoe.

715 Demonstrate to a qualified water safety person your ability to tip a canoe in deep water, right it, and get aboard.

716 Paddle 5 miles in 1 day with equal time spent in bow and stern positions. Do this with a partner.

In a sailboat:

717 Rig a small sailboat.

718 Demonstrate casting off, coming about, jibing, heading up.

719 Demonstrate sailing up to and securing at a mooring.

720 Build and sail an authentic model boat.

Winter Sports

801 Know and discuss safety measures and proper clothing for winter activities on snow and ice.

802 Remove the snow from your steps and walks, or driveway, after a storm.

803 Play snow games, such as fox and geese, statues, etc., for 4 hours in any month.

804 Make a lifesize snow or ice statue, alone or with your group.

805 Be a working member of a committee to plan and carry out an exhibit in snow sculpture.

806 Attend 2 winter picnics.

807 Coast, toboggan, snowshoe, or ski, for not less than 10 hours in 2 months.

808 Know the safety rules for roller or ice skating, and the proper care of your skates.

809 Demonstrate your ability to skate forward and backward, stopping and changing direction easily.

810 Help plan and carry out a family party in which everyone has an opportunity to roller or ice skate.

811 Skate forward and backward in dance position, with a partner.

812 Make and use a chart of safety rules for outdoor roller skating. Find a safe place for keeping your skates when not in use.

813 Demonstrate to skating instructor or other expert that you can perform well 3 figures on skates.

814 Perform 1 of the following turns in skating: Mohawk, Spread Eagle, 3-turn.

815 Participate in a skating (roller or ice) show or demonstration.

816 Make 6 ski turns, such as stem or snowplow.

817 Ski down a slope in good form, for 15 yards.

818 Demonstrate while skiing, the herringbone, side stepping, and kick turns to the right and to the left.

819 Show complete control in a downhill run on skis, and do at least 3 connected snowplow turns.

Progression in Outdoor Living

To be a real camper you need to learn to be at home out of doors. The following groups of activities will show you how to use the knowledge you have gained by earning Outdoors Craft honors—and have fun doing it. Some skills will be new to you; some are familiar but now that you know how, you can do them better.

Skills activities are arranged in steps, from easy to more difficult. You must complete one group of skills before you go on with the next.

Learn and practice the skills in your group, at day camp, or at your Camp Fire Girls resident camp. Do them as they fit into your regular group or camping activities. Keep a record of your progress by asking your guardian or camp counselor to initial and date each activity as you complete it, like this:

7-5-6	G.H.H.

You may wear the Fagot Finder and Trail Maker emblems on your ceremonial costume when you have completed the beginning steps and the activities listed under these two groups of skills. (Your guardian can secure them for you.) These skills will help you achieve Gypsy and/or Torch Bearer in Outdoor Living when you are a Junior Hi Camp Fire Girl!

Beginning Steps

Here are skills in outdoor living which you must have *before you start working* on Fagot Finder. These are some of the first things you will need to know to have fun and live skillfully out of doors. You and your group may enjoy doing these together. You'll find you are earning Outdoors Craft honors too!

— Describe the trees and birds you've spotted on your camp site, or in your neighborhood in any 3 days. Also find the Big Dipper in the sky.

— Show how to measure distance by paces.

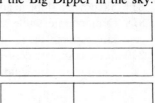

— Learn 2 kinds of knots and their uses.

— Talk with your group about safety rules and how to dress for hikes. With at least 6 others, plan and go on a 1- or 2-mile hike. Take picnic lunches. Plan food, clothing, destination, and first aid equipment.

— Learn and demonstrate the proper use and care of a jackknife. Make at least 1 simple item, or shavings for a fire.

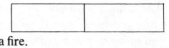

— Learn about kinds of wood for fires —tinder, kindling, firewood—softwoods and hardwoods. Learn how to make a woodpile. Gather the wood and make a woodpile.

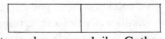

— Learn basic facts about fire building (see Chapter 13). Build and use the basic fire. First, clear a safe area for fire building. With at least 6 others, cook a simple one-pot dish. Plan menu and kapers.

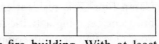

— Learn and demonstrate packing of a sleeping bag, or make a bedroll. Discuss use for an overnight trip.

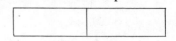

Fagot Finder— First Step

1. Learn the Conservation Pledge. Tell how you have tried to keep it.

2. Clear outdoor areas for fire building, cooking, eating, etc.

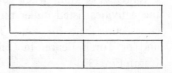

3. Use a jackknife to prepare 2 use-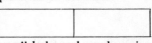
ful pieces of equipment. Demon-
strate the proper use of a saw for preparation of firewood.

4. Learn to build 2 additional kinds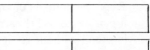
of cooking fires (crisscross, hunter-
trapper, etc). Use these for cooking 2 well balanced meals, using
different recipes and different methods for each meal. Plan the
cookout with at least 6 others.

5. Make lists of equipment needed for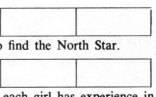
overnight. Include personal items.

6. Show how to whip the ends of a
rope. Show 2 additional kinds of
knots and their uses.

7. Learn and demonstrate how to read
a compass. With 7 others play a
game using a compass. Show how to find the North Star.

8. Plan and go on an overnight. Cook
at least 2 well-balanced meals out-
doors. Rotate responsibilities so that each girl has experience in
planning, cooking, fire building, cleaning up, and taking fire precautions.

Trail Maker— Second Step

(Complete the Fagot Finder before you start this.)

1. Learn square, diagonal and sheer
lashing. Lash a simple item.

2. Learn how to pitch a pup tent or a
small wall tent.

3. Learn and demonstrate the use of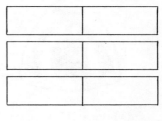
a hand axe. Saw and chop wood
for a meal.

4. Learn 2 additional cooking fires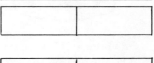
(trench, reflector, etc.). Use these
to cook 3 outdoor meals, with new recipes and new methods. Plan
with at least 6 others.

5. Make a simple map of a camping
area, using a compass.

6. With at least 6 others help to make a new path in camp or in a wooded area, protecting natural resources.

OR

With at least 6 others take responsibility for improving public property by clearing paths, checking erosion, planting, etc.

7. Pack camping equipment so that it can be carried. Learn about storing food without refrigeration.

8. Plan and carry out a 1- or 2-night camping trip. Cook at least 4 well balanced meals outdoors.

Gypsy—Third Signpost

When you have completed Trail Maker and are at least 12 years old, you may work on the Gypsy skills. These are shown in the *Book of the Junior Hi Camp Fire Girls*.

Symbolism of Outdoor Living Emblems:

Fagot Finder

Kettle, crane and fire symbolize beginning skills in outdoor living.

Crane and kettle, royal blue; fire, orange.

Trail Maker

Person, trail and trail markers symbolize progress on the trail, and growing skills.

Girl, green; trail, yellow.

The Swimming Emblems

Do you want to test your swimming skill? Go to your nearest American Red Cross (ARC) chapter or consult a Red Cross Water Safety Instructor about taking their swimming instructions. You will be:

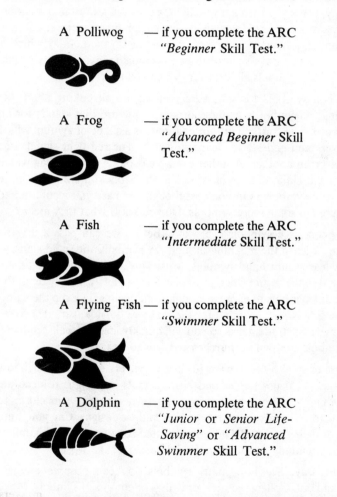

A Polliwog — if you complete the ARC *"Beginner* Skill Test."

A Frog — if you complete the ARC *"Advanced Beginner* Skill Test."

A Fish — if you complete the ARC *"Intermediate* Skill Test."

A Flying Fish — if you complete the ARC *"Swimmer* Skill Test."

A Dolphin — if you complete the ARC *"Junior* or *Senior Life-Saving"* or *"Advanced Swimmer* Skill Test."

You may wear emblems of the swimming symbols illustrated here on your bathing suit or ceremonial costume. These may be ordered by your guardian through the council office, or from the Camp Fire Girls, Inc., Supply Division. *Plunge in!*

CHAPTER 9

SYMBOLISM AND YOU

Symbols Are Everywhere

Symbols are everywhere! Think for a moment how many you have seen today. Have you seen a traffic light, a cross on a church, our American flag, a red feather? Have you drawn a stick figure picture, a $ sign, or a pumpkin, a heart, or a turkey, depending on the holiday which is nearest? If so you have seen or drawn symbols today. But this is only a start. You see symbols almost everywhere you look.

What is a symbol? Let's be sure that we are all talking about the same thing. A symbol is a shape or simple picture that stands for an idea or word. The traffic light, for example, is a shape or symbol which both drivers and pedestrians learn to watch. The red light signals one thing, the green another. Another example is our American flag which stands for the United States of America. Probably you are much more familiar with symbols than you first thought. In case you would like to check, here are some more symbols. Do you know what they mean?

Most people see symbols every day. Before we can pass a driver's test we must learn the meaning of highway symbols and hand signs. A secretary learns shorthand symbols. Musicians use symbols to tell them what sound to make and whether to play fast or slowly, loudly or softly. Artists paint symbols to express thoughts and feelings. (Even the painting of the tree is just a symbol for the real tree outside, isn't it?) Manufacturers design trademarks so you will quickly identify their products. Many symbols are used in churches and synagogues.

The use of symbols to express ideas is very, very old. Your neighbors around the world use flower and bird symbols or designs to decorate their clothing and household things. These neighbors seem closer to you when you can recognize the symbols in their designs. Can you think of some of their symbols? They are repeated sometimes, like a familiar tune. They remind you of their special corner of the world.

A Symbol Day: See how many symbols you can observe all day, indoors and out. Collect pictures, drawings or cutouts of symbols. Make a group symbol scrapbook or a symbol exhibit to share your discoveries with others.

Step 1: Decide the date of your group's special Symbol Day. It might be a regular meeting day, a holiday, or Camp Fire Girls birthday.

Step 2: Before the big day watch out for symbols in magazines and newspapers which you can cut up. Take a treasure hunt through them. Make sketches, paint, draw or cut out different kinds of symbols. Watch for symbols wherever you are—as you go to school, on buildings, in your church or synagogue, as you watch television.

Step 3: Symbol Day arrives. Take to your meeting all the symbols you've collected—pictures, drawings, lists with simple line sketches. Everyone compare symbols. How many different ones has your group collected?

Make a guessing game of identifying the symbols. Try to dramatize your symbols. Act out words or symbols by using hand signs and drawings symbols in the air (air pictures!).

Step 4: Make your group's symbol scrapbook. The girls who like to draw or paint can Seek Beauty by making a cover for the book. Decorate it with symbols in color. Will you put the Camp Fire names of the girls in your group, your guardian, and your group name in this book? Add your symbolgrams when you have made them?

A Symbol Hike: Plan and go on a symbol hike with your group and guardian. How many symbols, hand signs and symbol sounds can you observe? Plan with your group when and where you'll hike. Will it be on a meeting day, on a Saturday, or on a special holiday? Will you take a fruit snack to munch on the way? Be sure to take a notebook and pencil to jot down and sketch your discoveries.

Symbol Sounds: Have you ever thought of the church bell, the school bell, the fire alarm, the automobile horn as a symbol sound? What does the chirping of the first robin say? What does the rooster say when he crows? Or the dog when he barks? What does the whistle mean in a game, at the factory, when the policeman blows it? What does the wind tell you when it howls, when it rustles softly on a warm day, when it blows the fallen leaves? What other symbol sounds can you name?

Hand signs are symbols too. They tell us something without using words or pictures or sounds. How many can you think of right now? Who uses hand signs besides the traffic officer, the automobile driver? Find out how the program director in a radio or television studio uses silent hand signs to send messages to the performers.

Indian Symbolism

Because Camp Fire Girls was started in the United States, we naturally look for inspiration to our first really native folk art—that of the American Indian. We want to honor this important part of our country's heritage. Camp Fire Girls have found a special and very interesting way of doing this. The beauty and color of American Indian crafts and costumes, the picture symbols used to tell stories and "talk", and the way Indians lived are fun for Camp Fire Girls to learn about. This lore is found throughout the Camp Fire program. The ideas for writing in Indian symbols, your symbolgrams, your Camp Fire names, your ceremonial meetings (which Indians called "council fires"), and your ceremonial costume all came originally from American Indian lore.

You'll have fun learning about the symbols of the American Indians. They are beautiful in their color, design, and meaning. Some are simple line drawings, like a triangle for a tepee or a heart. They were used in every part of the Indian's life.

Have you ever walked in the grass in soft brown Indian moccasins? How soft the leather felt on your feet! How quietly you could walk! Or have you ever seen some of the suede leather moccasins decorated by th Indians with lovely beaded designs? Did you notice the colors in the bead work, and the symbols of flowers and leaves formed by those tiny beads? The American Indians made beautiful things, decorating them with colors and symbols and designs. Their traditions are carried on by the fine Indian craftsmen today.

THE YEAR IN MOONS

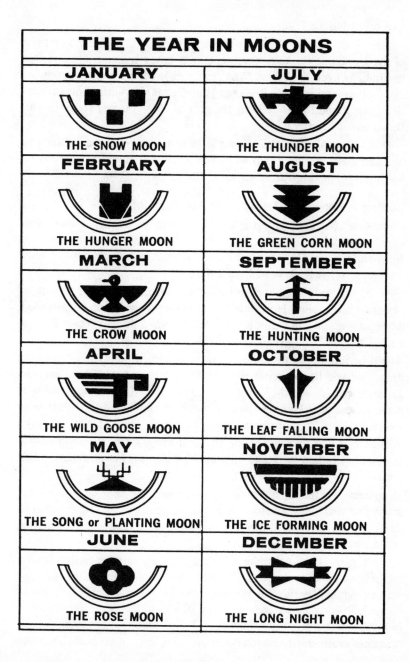

JANUARY	JULY
THE SNOW MOON	THE THUNDER MOON
FEBRUARY	AUGUST
THE HUNGER MOON	THE GREEN CORN MOON
MARCH	SEPTEMBER
THE CROW MOON	THE HUNTING MOON
APRIL	OCTOBER
THE WILD GOOSE MOON	THE LEAF FALLING MOON
MAY	NOVEMBER
THE SONG or PLANTING MOON	THE ICE FORMING MOON
JUNE	DECEMBER
THE ROSE MOON	THE LONG NIGHT MOON

Exploring Indian Trails

American Indians lived at one time (some still do) in many parts of the United States. City pavements may cover Indian trails now, but the Indians lived there first. What tribes of Indians lived in your state? Did Indian families once live near your Camp Fire Girls camp? Sometimes you'll find Indian relics in the ground. Did you ever see or find an Indian arrowhead?

Would you like to know about the Indians who lived near where you live and go to school? It would be fun to do Indian crafts like weaving and pottery-making. You can learn Indian dances too.

Getting to Know Your Friends, the American Indians

Imagine that your group is an Indian family: mother, father, children, grandparents. Maybe there are cousins or aunts and uncles, too. Imagine that you are living right there in your own neighborhood, only it's years and years ago, in Indian days.

What did your neighborhood look like then? Were there forests or plains or mountains? How did your little family live? You needed food and clothing, and the children wanted to make things. What did you eat? Where did you get food? How did you cook it?

It'll be interesting to find out how your Indian family lived in those days. Did you have a tepee or a bark house, or what? Where did you get materials for a home? How did you dress? Did you travel from one place to another? Did the wild animals and plants and the forest help you with food, clothing, even transportation?

How can you find out about all these things? Try reading aloud a story about Indian boys and girls and families who once lived in your area.

Is there an Indian museum or an Indian site that you and your group can visit? Plan a trip to see costumes, crafts, rugs, Indian pottery. Look for all kinds of things Indian boys and girls and their parents made and used and loved.

An Indian cookout or picnic is fun, right where your Indian family might have lived. Act out all the things they did, like hunting, fishing, making pottery, caring for papooses, cooking and dancing.

Making and Using Indian Things

Indian crafts are interesting and fun to learn. You'll probably need to make some things to use in a puppet show or in Indian dances. Here are a few ideas:

For clothes: Make simple garments from unbleached muslin, dyed, or from burlap (maybe potato bags or feed bags, washed). Decorate them with shells, seeds, fringes or "beaded" designs made with paint or crayons. Try making headbands from cloth or paper and decorate them. Remember, Indian women didn't wear eagle feathers. The feathers were often worn by men.

Dwellings: Make a dwelling large enough to use, an Indian tepee with poles, burlap or old sheets. Paint it with large colorful symbols.

Cradleboard: Some Indian mothers carried their babies in a cradleboard. Make one of wood. Make the papoose of cloth, stuffed with cotton.

Masks and rattles: For your Indian dances you can make masks from brown paper bags. See Chapter 15. For rattles, try to get gourds (not shellacked). Hang them up to dry. They will get lighter and lighter. After a few weeks they'll be so dry the seeds will rattle. Paint them with bright symbols. Or use small brown paper bags; decorate them with symbols. Put a few pebbles inside and gather the top of the bag around a short stick for a handle. Tie tightly and shake!

Telling Stories with Indian Picture-Writing

The Indians drew pictures for words. They drew pictures of things and people.

We call these pictographs or picture-writing. The Indians had their own names for the word-pictures. They painted them on bark or animal skins, stones, or sometimes on birchbark from fallen trees. They also painted records of their family on totem poles and on the inside walls of their bark homes.

Indians made their own paints—reds, greens, blues, and yellows—from grasses, juices of berries, colored earths, or dried plants and flowers ground into powder. Do you know what some Indians used for brushes? The spongy parts of buffalo bone.

Until Indian children went to school, they wrote in word-pictures too. They told stories with them just as we do when we write words. You can make a pictograph too; see how it might look on page 124.

What Some Camp Fire Groups Have Done

One group had an American Indian party, with Indian ideas for decorations, food, games, even Indian names for the guests. One girl told charming Indian legends as another girl accompanied her on an Indian drum she had made. Each girl had a part in the Indian songs and dances.

Another group visited an Indian craft shop and saw a wonderful collection of Indian baskets, woven beadwork, pottery bowls painted with symbols. There were woven Indian rugs with colored symbols, beaded moccasins, Indian dolls, Indian costumes and a chief's feathered headdress.

A third group made a miniature Sioux Indian village, complete with lakes, tepees, fires, skin racks, papoose boards, trees, and Indian men, women, children, and dogs! The girls also made dolls and dressed them in Indian costumes. They packed a surprise box of gifts for an Indian Mission and had fun giving service.

In still another group, the girls collected all the Indian symbols they could find of the different Indian tribes who had lived and still do live near them. They had an exhibit of these in the town library.

USE AMERICAN INDIAN SYMBOLS TO TELL A STORY . . . .

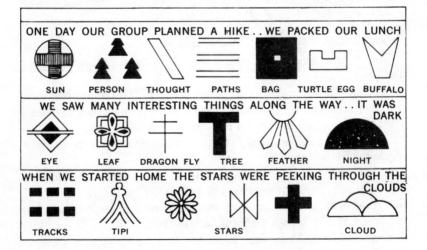

ONE DAY OUR GROUP PLANNED A HIKE . . WE PACKED OUR LUNCH

SUN   PERSON   THOUGHT   PATHS   BAG   TURTLE EGG   BUFFALO

WE SAW MANY INTERESTING THINGS ALONG THE WAY . . IT WAS DARK

EYE   LEAF   DRAGON FLY   TREE   FEATHER   NIGHT

WHEN WE STARTED HOME THE STARS WERE PEEKING THROUGH THE CLOUDS

TRACKS   TIPI   STARS   CLOUD

WAYS TO HAVE FUN WITH SYMBOLS

Can't you just imagine *clouds,* when you see several semicircles together? That is the way some Indians write it. And *rain* is a series of vertical (up and down) lines.

To help you get acquainted with symbols, here on the following pages are symbols you'll see most often. They have been enlarged and printed in outline form to help you hold symbols in your hands. Try drawing or tracing these symbols. Then cut them from brightly-colored construction paper. Make several sets for your group. Put each set in an envelope. Mount one or two sets on cardboard to use in games.

Symbol Stories

Tell stories or illustrate little poems with symbols. For example, look at the story of a hike told with symbols. Can you read it in symbols?

SYMBOL STORY OF A HIKE

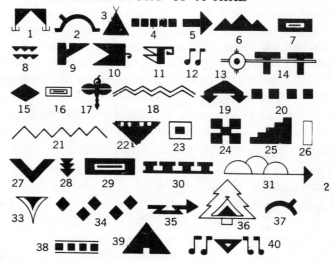

Key #1. This is the translation in symbols:

1 Saddle bag	15 Person	29 Eye
2 Morning	16 Eye	30 Skyband
3 Sunrise	17 Dragonfly	31 Clouds
4 Tracks	18 Water	32 Arrow
5 Arrow	19 Frog	33 Far-off rain
6 Mountain	20 Tracks	34 Tracks
7 Eye	21 Water	35 Speed
8 Dew	22 Hand	36 Tree with wigwam
9 Leaves	23 Bag	37 Afternoon
10 Bird	24 Rocks	38 Paths and tracks
11 Bird	25 Mountain	39 Tent
12 Note	26 Path	40 Notes and heart
13 Sun rays	27 Mouth	
14 Trees	28 Corn	

Key #2: This is the translation in English words:

"Leaving in the early morning we walked toward the distant mountains. We saw dew on the leaves and heard birds singing. The sun made rays through the trees. I saw a dragonfly near a stream, and a frog.

"We waded in the water and gathered pretty stones. We climbed a cliff and ate our lunch where we could see into the distance. Big white clouds were turning to rain so we ran quickly to a sheltering tree. Later we walked home singing happily."

Now, would you like to try writing a picture story of your own? If so, follow these four steps.

1. You must choose or compose a story. You might tell about one of your group's recent trips or projects, about something that happened at school, about a made-up Indian story, or anything you like. Just remember to make short sentences and to leave wide spaces between the lines and between the words.

2. Check to see what symbols would stand for the words and ideas that you used, and draw the symbols under or between the words.

3. Color the symbols with crayon or water color.

4. Send your story to a shut-in friend, to Camp Fire friends in another group, or to your pen friend.

If your group decides to write a story together, this can be interesting too. Every girl helps to write it. The story will probably be about one of the group's experiences or something about which all the girls can contribute. Remember to keep those sentences short! Next, each girl makes her own copy of the story, leaving enough space to be able to draw in symbols between or underneath the words. When each girl's story is completed, compare the symbols you used. What symbols did the other girls use? How many different symbols were used in all?

Here's another way to make a pictograph, which will look more like the Indians might have done.

1. Write your story, remembering to keep your sentences short.

2. Divide the story into parts. One or two girls can work out one idea, or a part of an idea. Then plan picture-words to tell that part of the story. When all are finished, you will be ready to put the parts together to tell the story with symbols.

3. Cut or tear a large sheet of wrapping paper or cloth into the shape of an animal skin.

4. Plan where the symbols will go, then sketch them in with pencil.

5. Color with poster paint or crayon. Or, glue in place symbols cut from colored paper or made from nature materials, to tell your story.

Now, think of something nice to do with your pictograph. Would you like to give it to your librarian? Or to someone who has helped your group? Or to a new group, to show them how to make pictographs? Or as a display or decoration to tell about Camp Fire Girls in your community? You'll be proud to say, "Our group made it."

A Symbolina Party

Have a Symbolina, a party with everything in symbols! Invitations, decorations, games, little prizes, and refreshments—all are made with symbols.

Try writing your invitations in symbols first, or send each girl an invitation decorated with the moon symbol for her birthday month. (The Indians called the months "moons.")

Birthday place cards are fun, again using each girl's birthday moon symbol for decoration. Or you can make personality place cards. Use a couple of symbols to stand for the things each girl likes or does. Give each girl duplicates of her personality symbols to match with her place card. Let her guess what her symbols mean and why you chose them. Choose symbols that will say nice things about each girl.

Personality place cards or name tags are easy to make. For example, a tree and a bird symbol could be for a girl who likes nature; symbols for rocks, flowers or stars could also be hers. Symbols for sun and person could be for a girl who always has a sunny smile. For someone who likes to ride horseback or travel, a symbol for stirrup could be combined with mountain or path.

Symbol *refreshments?* Bake cookies cut in symbol shapes. One group made cupcakes with symbol designs on the frosting. Another had cupcakes with plain frosting, and small cut-out symbols standing up straight on the top of each cake.

You can decorate your paper tablecloth and napkins with symbols. Cut and paste, or draw with Magic Markers. For the hostesses, make tiny aprons with symbol pockets or trimming. Plan symbol games and symbol prizes.

Symbol Games

Play two or three symbol games, using at least six different symbols. Choose eight or ten Indian symbols. Cut them out of colored paper. Mount two or three sets of these symbols on cards. Now you are ready for a game. Make up your own, or try

Symbol Scramble   This is similar to Fruit Basket, but uses symbols instead of names of fruit. Form a circle with one girl in the center. Number off by fours. All the ones are the same symbol. The twos are another and the threes another; the fours another. (Example: ones are *tree* symbols, twos are *hand,* threes are *person,* fours are *thought.)* It, in the center, holds a symbol up high. The girls who are that symbol exchange places while It tries to get one of their empty seats. If It does, she becomes that symbol. When It calls "Indian Symbols," everyone changes places

Symbolo is a game that Camp Fire Girls especially enjoy. Make a set of cards approximately 8″ x 10″, one for each girl. Rule into 9 or 16 squares, using ink or crayon. Paste, crayon or paint a different symbol in each square, following the idea shown here. Use different colors for the symbols. Make the symbols and the arrangement of symbols on each card a little different from those on any other card. Make a duplicate set of the individual symbols to match those on the cards.

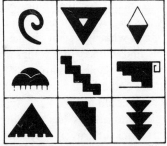

To play Symbolo: Each girl has a card on the table in front of her. One girl is game leader. She has the pile of symbols matching those on the cards. As she selects a symbol from the pile and holds it up, the girl who has one to match it on her card covers the square with a button or a kernel of popcorn. The one who first gets all her squares covered calls out "Symbolo" and wins the game.

Guess What   Divide the group into teams of 4 or 5 players each. Have a pencil and paper for each team. Number off by fours or fives. Leader calls all number ones to her. She whispers a symbol which they are to draw when they return to their team. They must draw it without saying a word. The first team guessing the correct symbol gets a point. Repeat with other symbols for the other numbers in the teams.

Jigsaw Cut symbol cards in two pieces and match them for partners. The couple matching and guessing their symbol first starts the next game.

Note: Would you and your group like to know even more about Camp Fire Girls symbols? Your guardian can order *Your Symbol Book* (Cat. No. D-75), or find it in the Camp Fire Girls council library.

Camp Fire Names
Choosing Your Own Name

In Camp Fire, another way of using symbols is in choosing a name for yourself. Yours can mean anything you want it to because *you* choose it! You will be happiest with your Camp Fire name if you first *think* and *talk* about what you want it to mean. It might stand for something you want to *become,* such as a fine swimmer, a teacher, an artist, a nurse—or an astronaut! Or it could mean something you want to *have:* a happy heart, a smile in your eyes, many friends. Choose a name from Indian words, or create a new name by combining parts of Indian or English words in a pleasant-sounding way. That is how our Camp Fire Girls special word, *Wohelo,* was made!

Suppose you want your Camp Fire name to mean, "I want to have lots of friends, so I'm going to try to be a good friend." You might choose *Tawasi,* which means friend, or perhaps you want your name to mean "I will keep trying until I can do things easily and well." You might take the two Indian words, *Luta,* meaning to hang on or stick to, and *Okihi,* meaning able to do or succeed. Put both words together. You have *Luta-Okihi.* Seems too long? Try taking parts of each word— *Lut-oki* or *Ki-luta,* or *Ta-kihi.* Choose the one with the most pleasing sound—*Lutoki, Kiluta, Takihi.*

Your Camp Fire name is used only in your group. Very few persons besides your own group, your guardian, and your family will know what your name means. It probably means something extra special to you. Your guardian will use it at group ceremonials when she calls you and the other girls into the circle to receive your honors and ranks.

Your Group's Name

Your group has a personality all its own. Think about what you want your group to stand for, and talk it over in the group. Look up Indian words and meanings. Choose your group name the same way you will choose your own names. Later you may want to make a group symbolgram, just as you will make your own symbolgram.

Designing Your Symbolgram

Your symbolgram, to be truly yours, is going to come from your own ideas. It says in colors and shapes what your Camp Fire name means to you. It may be something no one else knows about. A stranger admires your symbol for its beauty and color, but to you, it means something you want to do and be. So fit your symbolgram to the ideas in your Camp Fire name—and watch yourself grow to fit your name!

Making the Symbolgram

Have you ever tried making a monogram of your initials, fitting the letters together to make a design to use on your stationery and other personal things? Your symbolgram is something like a monogram, only it's a completely original design. Even the colors you use may have symbol meaning, too.

Here is one way to make a symbolgram. Start with the ideas you put into your Camp Fire name. Suppose your name means you love nature and outdoors. What in nature is most interesting to you? Birds, trees, plants? Jot down rough outlines of several bird symbols you like best. Try tree and leaf symbols too. Maybe you'll want to add sun and rain. From these you would choose the three or four you like best. Combine them to make your symbolgram.

After you have sorted out the ideas your name stands for, choose symbols to fit each idea. You can use Indian symbols, or symbols from the folk art of other countries, or be entirely original with modern symbols, if you wish. Then make colored cutouts of the symbols you've chosen (or find them in the sets of symbols your group made). Make them of different sizes, some large and some small. Try different symbols together. Overlap them a little so only parts of some symbols show. Try different color combinations. It's something like playing a chord of music, finding which notes sound best together.

Remember symbols can mean different things to different persons.

For example: the symbol for hand means the idea of "helping" to one girl. To another it means "making beautiful things with your hands."

Here's another example. One girl chose Woussicket for her Camp Fire name. It means "running brook." To her the brook symbolized happiness, purpose, helpfulness. She chose the brook with a bend in it for the unexpected adventures that lie ahead. She added the dragonfly for interesting things she might see, and because she loved nature. She used the corn symbol to show that the brook helps to make things grow.

Here are a few meanings given to nature symbols that girls have thought of and used in their symbolgrams. You'll think of other things, and other meanings. Use your imagination!

Some Symbol Meanings

Mountains: strength; stillness; seeing far ahead; climbing high; something to be overcome.

Trees: shelter; shade; food; protection; gracefulness; service; growing strong.

Path: adventure; courage; friendship; hiking; leading to a goal.

Star: goal; cheerfulness (twinkling); hope; leader; beauty; high aims.

Morning Star: new adventure; a new start.

Star and Path: camping; camping trips; outdoors.

Cloud: showers; flying; helping to grow; good crop; happy future.

Brook: cheerfulness; purpose; helpful; adventure; music, a merry heart; going places.

Lake: quiet; calm; thoughtful; swimming; canoeing; water; fish.

Arrow: swift; skill; speed; guidance; straightforwardness; sports; going straight to a goal.

Lightning: power; brightness; speed; do something fast.

Birds: travel; beauty; happiness; songs; color; flying; friendly; freedom.

Wings Outspread: protection; uplifted; flight.

Heart: generosity; love; sympathy; desire to do for others.

Hand: helpfulness; service; friendliness; artist; skill in making things.

Eye: seeking; understanding; appreciation; seeing beauty; discovery.

Thought: understanding; knowledge; thoughtfulness; wisdom; excellence in studies.

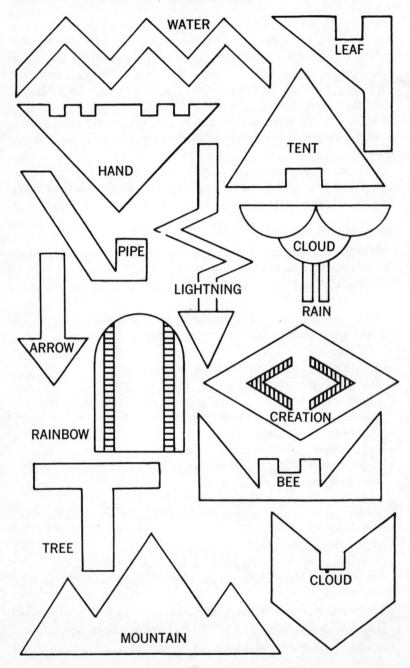

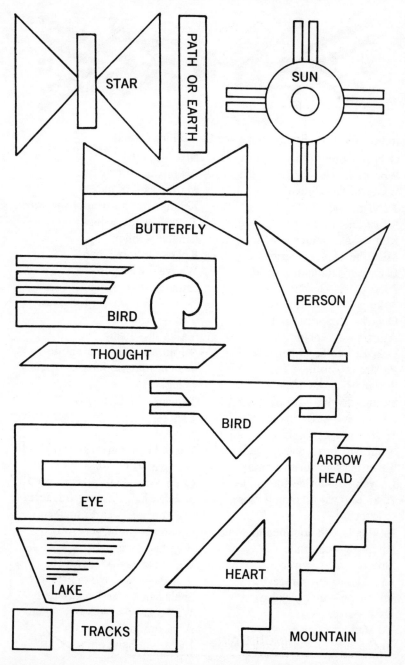

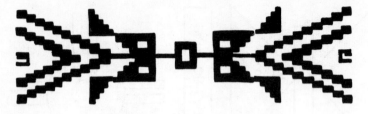

Indian Words—Suggestions for Camp Fire Names

O ki hi—able to accomplish
Woh do ke ca—skillful artist
Wa di ta ka—brave
Ta yi to—counselor
Wi ca ka—faithful
Kon za—to influence
Mi ni he ca—industrious
E ha wee—laughing maid
Pa si pi ka—leader
A ka ga—to make; sketch
O wa—to paint; sketch
A ma ya—to plant
O ki zu—to be united
Pa shu ta—to be a cook
Shu ma lua—to write
So an ge ta ha—strong heart
Ki nun ka—grow; flourish
Hashat u aya—assist each other
Tami—to busy oneself
Ta ki ma—to form a circle
Lu yan sti—inside the circle
A ki psa ya—standing close to-
　gether
Ek o le la—to continue to go up
Ki cu wa—comrade
Shle ta—to discover
I yo ki—to encourage
Mi no we—magic voice
Os sa—eyes
Yu-stan—to finish
In cha nan do—fish under water

Niye—to fly
A kin yan—to fly over
Ma nu ka—friend
Keema—in the face of the wind
Te pa—white, wings
Chippa—willow
Ko ki—little woman
Wa wa—wild goose
Mu me ga—to smile
Wish ka ga—robin redbreast
Tao—singer
Ya ka ni—I sing
Wi no ta—sing in a chorus
Wa cin ton—to have understand-
　ing
Ta wan ka—willing to try
Can te ya tin za—cheer up by
　words
Wa pi ki ya—arrange things well
Was pan ki ya—'baker
O da ko—alliance; friendship
A ki yu ha pi—carry together
Ma kah wee—earth maiden
O han pi—to be generous
E ce tu—just; right
Wa can ki ya—kind; loving
Tan da—love; honor; respect
Snah nah—merry-hearted
Wa he kta pa—pilot
A pa sun ta—to sew
Lu ta—to hang on; stick to

A pa denska—butterfly
I ki ca ga—to grow to something
Can te su ta—firm of heart
Wa han ka—do difficult things well
A ta ya—to go directly to anything
I yo pta—to go on; make progress
O kpe—assist in carrying a load
Ke ko uya—attempt more than once
Metkla—carry a burden
Ki ci cin—carry for another
U ya—to come, become, grow
O da kon ya—friendly
Za ni ka—healthy; well
Da kon ya—to be friendly with
Na hi—to paint
Yallani—mountain

Nena—mother
Si so ka—robin
Pi da ki ya—to make glad
Akita—try for
Ke ko—try
Ptanka—youngest sister
Do wan—to sing
Lo lua—sleep out of doors
Yo lo—snow
Ta wa ten ya—willing for anything
Ci—song
Lo la—to trust, believe in
Tchewa—to float like water birds
Ma ku al a—to pitch camp in the mountains
A o wa ki ya—band together for a purpose

Note: Are you interested in learning more Indian words? *The Name Book* (Cat. No. D-95) shows the English words and their Indian meanings. Your guardian can order it, or find it in the Camp Fire Girls council library.

Making Your Honor Bead Jewelry

You'll love the color, shape and feeling of the Seven Crafts honor beads. They'll always remind you of good times with your group.

You'll want to string your first honor beads to wear with your Camp Fire costume at group ceremonials. Then you'll plan how to decorate your jacket in all the colors of the Seven Crafts. Each bead means something learned, some service given, something achieved, and good times shared. It's not "How many beads do I have?" but "What do they stand for?" that counts! They are your personal record of progress in Camp Fire.

When you have more honor beads than will look well on your jacket, try making honor bead jewelry. You can wear it with your service costume alone, as well as with your ceremonial jacket. Don't wear honor bead jewelry with fancy dresses, plaids or prints; it just doesn't look well.

Because these are all earned, such beads should not be strung with other kinds of beads. Many nice combinations of colors and shapes can be made with honor beads. Elastic thread in various colors can be used for stringing beads. Tie the ends for a bracelet. As a fastener for necklace or bracelet, use a bone ring, covered with buttonhole stitch of the colored crochet cotton on which you string the beads. One of the long beads is slipped through the ring to fasten.

How to String Your Honor Beads

Here are illustrations of several ways of stringing your honor beads. Just follow these directions and look at the pictures:

A-1. The beads are strung on a single cord in any desired order. Pay attention to the size and shape of beads, as well as to the color of the beads and cord. Buttonhole stitch around the bone ring first. Then proceed with stringing.

A-2 and 3. These are double-strand methods of stringing. Begin with a long bead (as the fastener). Tie it in the middle of a long cord (see a). Use a needle on each end of the cord.

In A-2 an equal number of beads are strung on each thread. Then the cords are knotted together at b. Repeat until the strand is long enough. Sew on the bone ring at the end.

In A-3 a bead is strung on each cord. Then each needle runs through the opposite ends of the same bead (see c). You can vary this by changing the size of beads, such as in 3d.

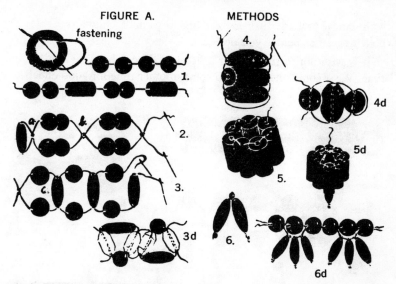

FIGURE A.   METHODS

A-4. This method is similar. A single strand is used with a needle on each end. Make long rows or links. Begin with one bead in the middle of the cord (cord is *not tied* together at all). Continue to string through opposite ends of each following bead. 4d shows this with beads of varying sizes. The cord shows in this kind of string so color should blend with the beads.

A-5. Continue the method in A-4 and lace both ends back through the first bead. This makes a circle. In 5d the cord was also strung through another middle bead to make a center.

A-6. Tie on tassels of beads as shown. In 6d the tassels are tied onto a loop of cord strung around the outside of a bead. The loop was one of a double cord, alternately strung outside of a bead.

Ideas for Making Honor Bead Jewelry

Many of the stringing methods shown in Figure A can be used for bracelets, necklaces, belts, lapel ornaments. See Figure B. With a small number of beads, the medallion can be made to look like a flower pin. It can be sewn on felt and pinned on a pocket. It can be sewn on the ceremonial jacket.

Use simple color combinations and shapes. The colors of the honor beads are so bright you'll find it looks better to put only a few colors together. A nice color combination might be the flame of Home Craft with the yellow of Business and the brown of Outdoors Craft. Try colors together before you decide.

It is wise not to try to wear all of your honor bead "jewels" at one time. Wear some one time, and some another time for good effects!

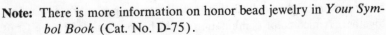

FIGURE   B   EXAMPLES

Note: There is more information on honor bead jewelry in *Your Symbol Book* (Cat. No. D-75).

Your Ceremonial Costume—Two Choices

Camp Fire offers its members a choice! As you know, there are two ceremonial costumes: the navy blue ceremonial jacket which is worn with your service costume, and the light brown ceremonial gown with brown suede leather fringes (which is often worn with moccasins and a headband). The group makes a much better appearance when all members wear the same ceremonial costume, either jacket or gown.

You will probably want to have your ceremonial jacket while you are becoming a Trail Seeker, but you will add to it and really decorate it when you are working toward Wood Gatherer rank and can sew on your symbolgram. Then you may want to have the ceremonial gown as you become a Fire Maker. Both are Camp Fire Girls ceremonial costumes. Most girls wait one more year, however, before getting their gown, so that they will not outgrow it. You would continue to wear either one as you go on into Junior Hi Camp Fire, and on some occasions, in Horizon Club.

Precious as your ceremonial costume—jacket or gown—becomes as you grow in Camp Fire, what it stands for is even more important. And what does it stand for? All the memories special to Camp Fire days—the lovely group ceremonials when you received your first few honor beads, the companionship of the girls in your group, the warm friendship of your guardian. Memories are different for each girl.

Your Ceremonial Jacket

Your ceremonial jacket is blue wool felt, made in sleeveless bolero style. The word "bolero" makes you think of Spain, doesn't it? Something similar to this type of jacket is a part of almost all folk costumes of the world. Several American Indian tribes wore a sleeveless jacket made of buckskin (and later of cloth). These were decorated with quill or bead designs. Our Camp Fire ceremonial jacket is adapted from the Indian buckskin jacket.

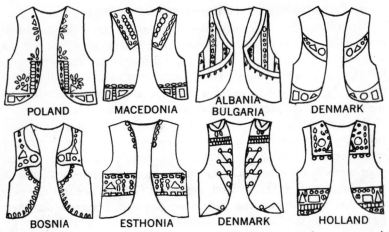

POLAND MACEDONIA ALBANIA BULGARIA DENMARK

BOSNIA ESTHONIA DENMARK HOLLAND

We also like to think of the girls (and boys, men and women too) of many other countries who have worn this sort of jacket. They decorated theirs with gay colors and folk art. Some decorations showed whether the wearer was a bride, a groom, a child or an older person. Often the decoration was the wearer's own choice. Sometimes the designs came down from grandparents and great-grandparents. Many symbolized the valley or mountain where the person lived.

It's fun to know that people in many other countries have worn this same sort of costume. It gives you sort of an international friendship feeling! You might decide to decorate your jacket in designs similar to those of the country your parents or grandparents came from. Sketches of some of the jackets worn in other countries are shown here. This type of jacket is so becoming to everyone that modern dress designers use it almost every season in some form.

FRONTS BACK TIE AREA

CLOUD HEART BUTTERFLY
FLOWER MOUNTAIN

Decorating Your Ceremonial Jacket

As soon as you have your jacket and you have created your symbolgram, you'll want to have a Decorating Bee at a group meeting. The girls bring their jackets and honors and symbols to the meeting. They help fit each other and compare plans for decoration. They try different ways of placing their honors on their jackets, and learn some fancy knots to use in making honor bead belts and bracelets.

It's best to make a paper pattern first. This will show how your design will look on your jacket. Your guardian will help you do this. Keep your decorations simple. Then as you earn new honors you'll have a place for them. They show how you are growing in Camp Fire.

Making a paper pattern

1. Cut two pieces of white or brown wrapping paper the shape of your ceremonial jacket, back and front. In pencil, sketch different ways you'd like to arrange your honor beads. Draw in outline the shape of your symbolgram. Does it fit a space on your jacket pattern? Try it in different ways. Select the one that you like best. Leave room at the top on the back of the jacket, so that no important part of the design will be hidden by the crossed logs and flame on your tie.

2. Make another pattern of your jacket out of dark blue or black construction paper, about the size of the paper (or 9″ x 12″). Make your symbolgram in color (crayon, paint, or colored paper cutout). Cut patterns of other symbol decorations you plan to use. Try them on the dark pattern. This will show you how your jacket will look when finished, and will help you decide about colors.

3. Select the pattern you like best. Pin it up in your room until your next meeting. If you still like it, you're ready to decorate your jacket. If you don't like it, try again!

Decorating with felt, yarn and honor beads

Felt is the most suitable material to use for decorations with your honors. It should be appliquéd (sewed) to the jacket. Wool yarn or colored thread is good. Glue or cement does not hold on felt. Use a blind running stitch; a decorative stitch can be used occasionally.

Be careful! Watch your color scheme. Don't clutter up your jacket with too many decorations. Choose from your earned honor beads the colors that will go best with your general color scheme. Use the others in a belt or other honor bead jewelry.

Symbol shapes made of felt in blue or contrasting colors can be beaded around the edge and appliquéd to your jacket. To be sure the designs fit, cut them of paper first and fit them to the jacket. Then cut felt designs from these patterns. Designs can also be put on with colored yarn in outline stitch, or press-on tape.

Your Ceremonial Gown

The Camp Fire Girls ceremonial gown is made in the style of the simple lovely buckskin gown once worn by Indian women of the Plains tribes. It is decorated with brown suede leather fringe, symbols, and your strings of honor beads. A headband with your symbol on it and brown leather moccasins are generally worn with the gown.

Decorating Your Ceremonial Gown

You start with your gown as a simple light brown dress with brown suede leather fringe. Very soon it becomes an ever-growing record of your progress and achievements in Camp Fire, shown by your Seven

Crafts honor beads, and your symbols; later perhaps you will add a brown suede leather collar and border.

A tuck under the hem will take care of those extra inches as you grow. The fabric hem of the gown should be about fourteen inches from the floor; this will bring the fringe to about ten inches from the floor.

Plan the decoration for your gown as carefully as you did for your jacket. You can use many of the same ideas for symbol shapes and borders, but belts, honor bead jewelry and costume jewelry are not worn with the gown. The gown itself allows more room for honor beads. They can be arranged in strings to hang from the collar. Handle your gown carefully so you will not lose the beads!

Every gown you see has a different story to tell. Some are quite plain; others are rich in decoration. This depends upon two things: how long the girl has been in Camp Fire and how well she has told her story in symbols and honor beads. No two gowns are ever exactly alike in decoration and beads. Each has happy memories for its owner.

As a Junior Hi Camp Fire Girl you will be proud of your own gown and you will have new symbols to add to it.

Things to Wear with Your Ceremonial Gown

Moccasins

A lovely gown may deserve a pair of moccasins to go with it. If you do not have moccasins, you would wear low-heeled brown shoes with your gown. You would not wear socks, they wouldn't look right with a ceremonial gown. You can make your own moccasins, or buy them. Try decorating them with beads and your symbol to match your headband.

A Headband

Your Camp Fire headband is suggested by the beautifully beaded headbands of the American Indians of the Plains tribes. There are many different ways you can make a headband. They are all interesting and fun. Naturally you will want to put your symbolgram on your headband, probably using the colors that you have used in decorating your ceremonial costume.

The illustration here shows how you can repeat your symbol for a headband or border design.

Make your headband to go all the way around your head. A full-length headband is much more attractive than a half-way one. Measure your head to get the right size. Draw your design on graph paper. Color it.

EXAMPLES OF REPEAT DESIGNS FOR HEADBANDS

Simple repeat design—note the background

Inverting the alternate design units—note zig zag effect and the star extended to suggest border

Ways to make your headband

A) Painting: Use oil or poster paints on leather or felt. A pinch of detergent added to poster paints will make them stick to leather.

B) Iron-on Tape: Cut symbols from colored iron-on tape. Press them onto the background with a hot iron.

C) Appliqué: This is sewing a cut-out design to a background. Cut symbols from felt to match the colors in symbolgram. Scraps are fine. Arrange design on background of felt. Other fabric or ribbon may be used.

D) Yarn: Try using yarn and a blunt tapestry needle on cross-stitch canvas or stiff net. This headband is reversible when it is finished. The design looks just as lovely on the back as on the front.

E) Beading: A beautiful way to make a headband is with beads . . . tiny colored seed beads woven on a bead loom. You can secure the loom, beading needles, thread, and beads from Camp Fire Girls Supply Division. Directions for weaving with beads come with the loom. They are also found in *Your Symbol Book*.

Note: Your guardian's friend, *Your Symbol Book* (D-75), has still more information on designing your ceremonial costumes and headbands.

CEREMONIALS IN YOUR GROUP

What is the loveliest part of Camp Fire? Your group ceremonials, of course. These are something very special. They are the occasions when you receive your honor beads or a Camp Fire rank. They are also the Camp Fire way your group can celebrate the new year or new members, Camp Fire Girls birthday, Thanksgiving, or other special times.

Where will you have it?

Have a ceremonial by candlelight in your regular meeting place. Make the room as attractive as you can. Have a few flowers, greens, or a small, bright mat or table cover.

Or have one out of doors if you can, around a small fire. Choose some lovely sheltered spot. Does someone have a nice back yard?

What do you wear?

Your service or ceremonial costume, of course, with any honors you have earned.

When do you hold ceremonials?

Whenever the group has some special time to observe, plan a ceremonial! Each group decides this for itself. Usually ceremonials happen every two or three months.

What do you do?

Often all the girls help their guardian plan the ceremonial. Other times a small committee makes the preparations.

You'll want to plan your ceremonial around a special theme. Then choose songs, poems, and spoken parts for lighting the fire or candles that relate to the theme.

Suggested Program for a Group Ceremonial

Wohelo Call: This is a greeting given by the guardian to the girls as they are about to enter the circle at the opening of the ceremonial. (You'll want to learn this before the ceremonial. The word, Wohelo, is sung in the key of C, on the notes E, G, and E. The accent is on the middle syllable.) The girls answer in the same way. The call may be given twice, the second time as an echo, or three times, the last time softly.

Entrance of the girls, singing, or quietly to other music.

Handsign of the Fire: A sign of greeting given first by the guardian and answered by the girls. It recalls the American Indian's sign language. All then sit in a circle around the fire or the candles. (To give the handsign: left hand, palm up, in front of you, waist high. Right hand, palm down on left hand. Slowly lift right hand directly upward, following curve of an imaginary flame until arm is above your head. Index finger should be pointing straight upward, other fingers of right hand curled softly toward palm. You are really picturing our Camp Fire Girls insigne in gestures.)

Group singing: Select one or two songs from this book; add others if you wish.

Lighting of the fire or the candles: Adapt a suggested ceremony; or better still, write your own words; put them into verse if you can.

The Camp Fire Girls Law: Say it or sing it all together.

Roll Call: Here you will use your Camp Fire name sometimes telling what it means to you. Or, girls answer by reading a very short poem they like or one they have written. Another way is to tell of some Camp Fire activity they have done. Still other times you may simply answer "Kolah," an Indian word meaning "friend."

Receiving new members: Someone might explain the meaning of your group name. Have a little welcome speech. Sing a cheer to the new members.

Awarding of Honors and Ranks: Your guardian may ask you to tell how you earned an interesting honor, or you could act out how an honor was earned. Awarding rank, of course, is very special. Your guardian will have a ceremony for this. (Note to your guardian: see the *Handbook for Guardians.*)

More group singing: Perhaps you'll sing to the girls who have been awarded a rank; or just sing together some favorite Camp Fire or folk songs. Good singing adds beauty to your ceremonial.

Your guardian's talk: This will be nice to remember!

Fire or Candle Extinguishing Ceremony: (See following suggestions.)

Closing songs, and a quiet exit.

Suggestions for Candle or Fire Lighting Ceremonies

Three girls who are to light the Wohelo candles, or the fire, come forward. The guardian lights her taper, and from it lights that of each in turn, for the lighting ceremony. Here are various suggested wordings.

Ceremony A—

First girl: "I light the light of Work."

Group: "We glorify work because through work we are free. Wohelo means Work."

Second girl: "I light the light of Health."

Group: "We hold on to health because through health we serve and are happy. Wohelo means Health."

Third girl: "I light the light of Love."

Group: "Love is the joy of service so deep that self is forgotten. Wohelo means Love."

All sing: "Wohelo for Aye."

Ceremony B—

First girl: "I light the light of Work, for Wohelo means Work." She

then lights one large candle (or the fire), and says alone or with
the group:
"We glorify work
For work well done is joy.
We work to be free, and to create,
We work for the joy of working
And because we are free.
Wohelo means Work."

She remains in place while the other two girls light their candles.

Second girl: "I light the light of Health, for Wohelo means Health.
We hold on to health
Because through health we serve and are happy.
We care for the health and beauty of our persons
For the body is the temple of the soul.
Wohelo means Health."

Third girl: "I light the light of love, for Wohelo means Love.
Love is comradeship
And motherhood and fatherhood
And all dear kinship.
Love is the joy of service so deep
That self is forgotten.
Wohelo means Love."

All three girls take their places in the circle at the same time.

Ceremony C—For a ceremonial on Friendship, Service, Citizenship:

First girl: "I light this candle to Friendship.
May its spark keep alive the friendships we make in Camp Fire
and hold them for the years to follow."

Second girl: "I light this candle to Service.
May we always know the joy and contentment
That comes from lending a hand to others."

Third girl: "I light this candle to Citizenship.
May its flame ever burn bright, warming our hearts
With love toward our fellowmen and hope of peace
For all nations."

LINDA MARSH, Camp Fire Girl
Canton, Massachusetts

Ceremony D—For a ceremonial when parents are present:

First girl: "I light the light of Home. In its light we see home treasures—sunlit rooms, a book or two, a glowing hearth, some
flowers, and shining dishes on a table. There is a friendly door that
opens wide to welcome every guest, and opens outward toward
the onward trail.

Burn brightly, flame of Home."

Second girl: "I light the light of Home Friendships. It shines upon
the broken dolls, the battered toys, the foolish jokes, the merry
laugh, the look of sympathy, the helpful word. Its beams shine
gently for our disappointments, gaily for our joys.

Flame of Home Friendships, burn long."

Third girl: I light the light of the Onward Trail. This is the flame
of courage and of seeking. It shines for racing clouds and sun
and rain, for song of birds, for winter's silver, autumn's gold;
sometimes, perhaps, for weariness and mists upon a distant hill.
It is a beacon and we follow where it leads.

Flame of the Onward Trail, burn true."

Fourth girl: (She takes an unlighted torch, holds it for a moment in
the flame of each candle, and from it lights the tall candle in the
center.) "In this center candle there shines the light of Home, of
Home Friendships, and the Onward Trail. Clear and true and
high its beams shine forth. It burns for you, our parents. You have
tended the light of Home that it might glow within our hearts and
become dearer as the days go by."

A Suggested Extinguishing Ceremony

Three girls extinguish the candles. The guardian gives to each girl
in turn the candle snuffer. (For an outdoor fire use water or sand.) The
whole group may say the last four lines of each verse.

The first girl says: "I extinguish the light of Work." She extinguishes
the flame, then says alone or with the group:

"Wohelo means Work.
Though the flame we extinguish
Yet the symbol remains;
In our hearts is the glory
And the freedom of workers.
Go we forth then with gladness

To show unto others
The thought of Wohelo
Translated to service."

Second girl: "I extinguish the light of Health.
Wohelo means Health.
May the flame that we lighted, its message leave with us,
A message of beauty
And of health to be treasured.
Go we forth then with gladness
To show unto others
What Camp Fire has taught us—
The keen joy of living."

Third girl: "I extinguish the light of Love.
Wohelo means Love.
And its flame ever burns;
Nor need we the candle,
For heart-deep its fire,
Its sweetness and power.
Go we forth then with gladness
To show unto others wherever they need us
A love that will fail not."

A Ceremonial Without Candles or Fire

It's not always possible to have a fire or use candles, so let's be original. Try this: use small colored balloons, symbolizing gaiety, adventure, ambition, etc. The first girl says, "I bring to our ceremonial this symbol of gaiety." She anchors the balloon in the center of the circle and finishes what she wants to say. And so on with the others. Leave the balloons there to float and pull at their moorings during the ceremonial. At the close set them free as symbols of hopefulness and freedom. (Gas-filled balloons will really float high away.) This is a nice ending for an outdoor ceremonial.

Props for Ceremonials

You'll be planning a ceremonial before long. But that won't be the only one. Your group will look forward to having them this year and the next and the next.

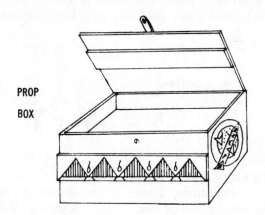

PROP
BOX

Why not start with a Prop Box or ceremonial chest and store your smaller ceremonial treasures in it? A heavy corrugated paper box with a tape hinge cover is good, but a light-weight wooden box is better. Perhaps you can convert an old fruit crate by careful sanding and covering. Would the dads like to help? Then paint and decorate it with colorful symbols. The chest will become a Camp Fire heirloom! You'll probably want to pass it on to a younger group some day.

Here are some of the things the chest might hold:

Poems, Songs, and Ideas to use in a ceremonial. Collect your favorites. Perhaps these would be best kept in a notebook or folder.

Your Wohelo Candles Because it's not always possible to have a ceremonial around a fire, candles are often used. Tall slow-burning candles are best. Use good straight ones. Any number and any colors may be used, depending upon your ceremony and your theme. After each use, wrap them and put them in tubes if possible so they will not bend or break.

The Taper This is a smaller candle used for lighting other candles. To avoid using matches, this is lighted by your guardian and handed to the girls as they light the candles or fire.

Candle Protectors To keep the hot wax from dropping on your fingers, you can make protectors of cardboard. The first one shown here is simply a circle with two criss-cross slashes cut in the center. As the candle is inserted, the part of the cardboard that is bent down helps to keep it firmly in place. The square holder is more decorative. Its points are finished with a bead, as shown. Decorate with symbols.

Candle Extinguishers Perhaps your group has a real candle snuffer. If not, make a substitute. A cream dip, handle bent at right angles to the cone and painted, will be fine. Tongue depressors stained brown or decorated with symbols are also good. To one end attach a thong or cord with a few bright beads. Or model some small thimbles or very tiny bowls out of self-hardening clay; paint and decorate. This is fun to do! To use, simply set them like small caps on the lighted candles.

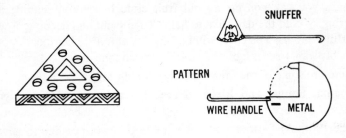

Candle Board for Center Candles A Wohelo triangle, made of wood about two inches thick and measuring about 12″ or 14″ on each side is good. If there are holes for several candles it will permit use of more than three candles. This is easy to carry. It may be stained, carved a bit, painted or sandpapered and varnished. How would your dads like to help your group make one of these?

Mats When ceremonials are held out of doors it is comfortable to have a mat to sit on. Ceremonial mats or pillows may be woven of reeds or cotton yarn warp, or cut from spongex and covered with felt or sturdy sailcloth or oilcloth. Try putting a stencil or appliqué of your personal symbolgram on this. Add small tapes so you can carry it easily.

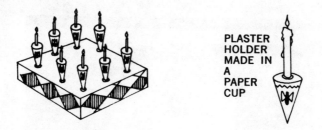

PLASTER
HOLDER
MADE IN
A
PAPER
CUP

New Member Candlestick For a ceremony welcoming new members, decorate a box with the symbol for persons (or another symbol) around the edge. Make holes in the top. Place cone-shaped candle holder in each hole. Cone-shaped candle holders are made by filling a pyramid-shaped paper cup with plaster of Paris. Why cone-shaped? Look up one of the symbols for "person" and you will see! Grease the end of a candle. Insert it in the plaster of Paris until it hardens. Then remove the paper and the candle.

Other Props Other things you might add to your ceremonial chest include a small rug or table cover to put under the candlesticks. This will add color and interest (and it will protect the table). Also an attractive Indian basket or bowl to hold honor beads and insignia of rank, matches in a safe tin box, and a pencil. Perhaps your group has individual candle holders too. These could go in the chest.

What Is a Council Fire?

The words ceremonial and council fire, in Camp Fire Girls, really mean the same. But when several groups gather together for a ceremonial, this is most often called a council fire. Three or more groups may wish to hold a council fire together once every year or two. This is an impressive occasion. It helps you see that Camp Fire Girls is much larger than your own group.

CHAPTER 11

CAMP FIRE GIRLS SING

Is yours a singing group? It will be as you try some of these Camp Fire songs and enjoy singing them together. Singing is a nice way to help new members feel they really belong to the group. It is fun to sing with other groups, and with your parents when you invite them to a special meeting.

The following songs were written especially for Camp Fire Girls. In *Songs for the Camp Fire Girls* (Cat. No. D-90) are even more of these songs. Try a new one every little while.

Your group will enjoy many other kinds of songs, too—lullabies, rounds, folk songs, patriotic songs, and action songs. Folk songs come from every country. Many have never been written down but are sung and loved and have been passed on from one generation to another. In *Music Makers* (Cat. No. D-79) you will find a collection of these beautiful songs that are fun to sing. Choose your favorites from this chapter and from the two books named here. Soon yours will be a singing group!

THE CAMP FIRE GIRLS LAW

Slowly

Wor - ship God (Hm - m - m - m)

a tempo

Seek beau - ty, give serv - ice, and

know - ledge pur - sue. Be trust -

worth - y ev - er in all that you do.

Hold fast on - to health and your

work glo - ri - fy. And you will be

hap - py, In the Law of Camp Fire.

WOHELO CHEER
Music from Aloha

Wo - he - lo for aye, Wo - he - lo for aye,

Wo - he - lo, Wo - he - lo, Wo - he - lo for aye!

Wo - he - lo for Work, Wo - he - lo for Health,

Wo - he - lo, Wo - he - lo, Wo - he - lo for Love.

OH, WE CHEER

Admont Clark

(Use also as a cheer to new members, a person or camp)

Oh, we cheer, Oh, we cheer for Wo - he - lo,

For our com - rades and friends so true.

And our loy - al - ty ev - er shall lin - ger,

Oh, Wo - he - lo, we sing to you.

WOHELO CALLS

OH, WOHELO

OH, STEP ALONG

Words and Music
Dorothy Neece Martin

Oh, step a - long in the Camp Fire way, And sing a
song, An - y mer - ry lay will make our work mere - ly
seem like play, And hap - py tasks can soon be done.
We like to cook and sew and hike a - long as al-ways
know - ledge we pur - sue. Hold on to health and stand up
straight and strong, Come on now girls, Let's step a - long.

PROCESSIONAL

(Kahinto Kamya)

Words & Music by

HELEN GERRISH HUGHES

Moderato con moto e impressivo

We
The

come, we come to our coun - cil fire With
lit - tle twink - ling stars on high, Are

meas - ured tread and slow To
whis - p'ring na - ture lore While

light   the fire   of   our   de - sire   To
all   a - bout   us   the   soft   winds sigh   And

light   the fire   of   Wo —   he - lo
Great   Wo - kan —   da   Watch — es   o'er.

slower

Wo —   he - lo   Wo —   he - lo.
Wo —   he - lo   Wo —   he - lo.

RESPONSES FOR FIRE LIGHTING

Mary Jeffries

Flame of work, burn glad, burn strong! Work that builds
Flame of Health, burn clear, burn bright! Glo - ri - fy
Flame of Love, burn warm, burn high! Kin - dle a

rit. gradually

beau-ty is done with song! Flame of glad work, burn strong!
Work with your joy - ous light. Flame of Health, burn bright!
fire that shall nev - er die. Flame of Love, burn high!

Mildred Littlefield

Burn, flame, bright - ly glow: Burn thou for Wo - he - lo.

1st ending   *2nd ending*   *3rd ending*

Burn, flame, burn. Burn, flame, burn. Burn, flame, burn.

NOW OUR COUNCIL FIRE BURNS LOW

Mary Doctor

Now our Coun - cil fires burn low; Wo - he - lo,
God our Guard - ian up a - bove, Wo - he - lo,

Wo-he-lo. Off to slum-ber soon we'll go; Wo-he-lo,
Wo-he-lo. Thank Thee for work, health and love, Wo-he-lo,

Wo-he-lo. Stars a-bove us soon will peep,
Wo-he-lo. Grant us, Fath-er, this we pray,

Watch-ing o'er us while we sleep. God, our Fath-er,
Bless all Camp Fire girls for aye; Thank Thee for an-

2nd verse ending

will us keep; Wo-he-lo, Wo-he-lo.
oth-er day. Wo-he-lo, Wo-he-lo, Wo-he-lo.

CEREMONIAL SONG

Sara Jamison

Come all ye Camp Fire mai - dens,
Come then and let us name it,

Sing as we ga - ther here,
Spir - it of Wo - he - lo,

Tell of your fun and la - bors
Whis - per it soft - ly o - ver

Fine

Tell of friend - ships dear.
as we home - ward go.

Sing of the joy that is

yours when you earn your hon - ors

Sing of the thrill as your

D. C.

friends go on - ward too.

CLOSING SONG

Words and Music by Clara Hallard Fawcett

Now our camp fire fa - deth,

Now the flame burns low,

Now all Camp Fire maid - ens to

slum - ber land must go. May the

peace of the lap - ping wa - ter, the

peace of the still star - light, The

peace of the fire - lit for - est be

with us through the night, The

peace of our fire - lit fac - es be

with us through the night.

RECESSIONAL

Words & Music by

HELEN GERRISH HUGHES

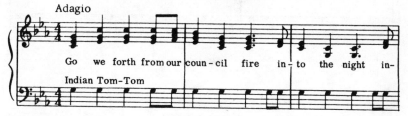

Adagio

Go we forth from our coun - cil fire in - to the night in-

Indian Tom-Tom

to the night. In our hearts re - newed de - sire

Burn - ing bright   Burn - ing bright   Love - li - ness of

thought we've found   warmth and friend-ship's love.

For - est still - ness clos - es round Sky and stars a -

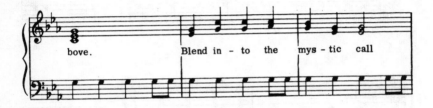

bove. Blend in - to the mys - tic call

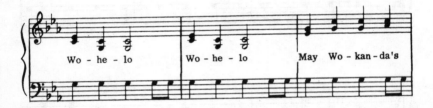

Wo - he - lo Wo - he - lo May Wo - kan - da's

bless - ing fall up - on us as we go.

FIRE MAKER'S DESIRE

Donna L. Brady

Melody

As fuel is brought to the fire, ___ So I pur-pose to

bring ___ My strength My am - bi -tion My heart's de - sire, My

joy and my sor - row ___ To the fire of hu - man-

kind; For I will tend As my fa-thers have tend-ed And my fa-ther's

fa-thers since time be-gan The fire that is called The love of

man for man, The love of man for God.

Part 3

ALL ALONG THE WAY

HOMEMAKING

One of these days you'll have a home of your own. You'll put into practice, and build on, many of the things you have been doing with your family and in Camp Fire while you were growing up. And wherever you live, now or "someday," love and kindness make your home your most important place. How can you learn to be a good homemaker?

Live the Camp Fire Girls Law

Worship God With your family worship regularly, and take part in the activities of your church or synagogue. Help your family enjoy the wonder of God's work in things around you: in starlit skies, in cool waters, in sunny days.

Seek Beauty Look for beauty in a flower, your home, the faces of your brothers and sisters and mother and father, in a household duty well done.

Give Service Open your eyes and see what you can do to help your family and your home. Then do it! Does that mean washing the dishes, running an errand, or watching over baby brother or sister? What else can it mean?

Pursue Knowledge Learn and share knowledge with those around you. Listen to music, share a good book, watch a television program together. Try a new recipe. Learn to use the iron or the oven.

Be Trustworthy Do you remember to hang up all your clothes? To put things away? To do that errand? Can the family depend upon you to do the things you've said you will?

Hold on to Health Help the family to have healthy meals by eating some of every part of the Basic Four foods, and by helping younger children to try new things. They want to do what you do. Have fun with the "Five-Minutes-a-Day-Fitness-Exercises," and ask your family to join in. Try doing them to recorded music.

Glorify Work That's easy, at home! Do your household jobs with a song and a smile. Set the table with a bit of imagination: add a few flowers, a tiny surprise favor or candlelight for a special occasion. Bake some cookies or muffins.

Be Happy Happiness is catching. Bring in the sunshine, and make yours a happy home.

At a group meeting . . . Put "Living the Camp Fire Girls Law" "on television." Ask each member in an interview how she lives the

LAW OF THE CAMP FIRE GIRLS.

Or talk about the Law, and each girl may then choose a point to act out. *Or* write the eight points on a large piece of paper. Your group can think of new ways to live them. Write these under each point.

Become a Charming Young Lady—Now!

"What do I need to do to be charming?" Just be your very best natural self. The following are good ways to judge.

Cleanliness. Do you take a sponge bath, a tub bath, or a shower daily? Do you wash your hands and scrub your nails with warm soap and water often, and always before meals? Are your nails short and attractive?

At a group meeting . . . have a "My Manicure, Please" session. Invite someone to show you how to care for your nails, and how to keep them short and shining. Make your personal manicure kit.

Hair. Do you brush it, brush it, brush it every day? That makes it shine! Do you wash it, and your brush and comb also, about every week? Be sure to rinse all the soap out. Do you like the way you wear your hair? Or would you like to have someone suggest a new hair-do that would make you look nicer?

At a group meeting . . . Invite someone to visit your group and discuss with you care of your hair, shampoos, and sub-teen hair styles. Demonstrate a shampoo. Try the hair styles.

Teeth. That Camp Fire smile makes you sparkle, so take good care of your teeth. Eat Basic Four meals. Brush your teeth after eating. Visit your dentist regularly. Show him how you brush your teeth. Ask him how you can keep them strong and white.

Eating, Sleeping, Exercise

Your good health is a precious thing. Ways which you can help protect this are to do these things *daily*.

Eat three Basic Four meals

Get eight or nine hours of beauty sleep
Do fitness exercises for five minutes daily
Enjoy an hour of Camp Fire sports and games
Get out in the fresh air and sunshine!

At a group meeting . . . Invite a nutritionist (a food specialist) to meet with your group. She will answer your questions about all kinds of food to eat and serve. Ask your guardian about writing to the National Dairy Council for illustrated booklets on all of these program tips.

Clothes Clothes are important! What is *most* important about them is how they are worn. How do you look when you go to your Camp Fire meetings, to school, or to a party?

—Are your clothes clean and neat? (No torn places or buttons off? Neatly pressed?) You can learn to take much of the responsibility for keeping your clothes ready to wear. Do you know how to wash clothes, iron, and mend? Do you take off good clothes before you play, and hang up clothes or put them away when you take them off?

—Are your shoes shined and the heels straight? Are your sneakers presentable?

At a group meeting . . . practice some of the skills necessary for the well turned out you. (This might be just the right time to practice your sewing, by doing a Needlework Guild project.)

Posture When you look in the mirror, is the picture a pleasing one? All the points which go to make a charming you are on parade: cleanliness, nails, hair, clothes, everything. And there's a final one—your posture. Make the most of you. Stand tall and sit still. Pretend you're a model . . . and you will be one, to your friends, to younger children, and to everybody who admires your fine posture.

At a group meeting . . . have a Posture Parade. Your group might invite someone to visit a meeting, to discuss and show you how to act out good posture. It's fun to learn how to walk onto a stage, stand up and sit down gracefully, and how to stand to look your best.

A New You?

Take another look in the looking glass. How do you score yourself now? Take a look every few months. See how your score improves!

Each "Yes" answer counts two points. "Sometimes" counts one point. Add them all up. What does your portrait in this "mirror" look like?

POINTS	YOU ARE . . .
41 to 44	Fairest of them all!
31 to 40	Lovely to look at!
21 to 30	Nice to know!
11 to 20	Sort of droopy?
1 to 10	Help! Help!

	YES	SOMETIMES
1. Do you keep your hair shining by good daily brushing and frequent shampoos?		
2. Are you proud of your hands with their short, clean nails?		
3. Do Camp Fire sports and games help you to "sit pretty" and walk tall?		
4. Does the family doctor give you a health examination once a year?		
5. Does what you eat include the Basic Four?		
6. Can you say "No, thank you," when candy or other sweets tempt you just before a meal?		
7. Does life look rosy because you get plenty of sleep?		

YES   SOMETIMES

8. Do sparkling teeth make it fun to smile?

9. Do your clothes, including your service costume, have that fresh-as-a-daisy look?

10. Do you avoid attention-getting manners, such as loud talking and interrupting others?

11. Can you be depended upon to carry out what you have agreed to do?

12. Are you careful not to find fault with other girls in your group?

13. Do you try not to repeat tales you hear about others?

14. Are you courteous to your friends, your family, and others?

15. Do you help newcomers feel welcome in your group, at school, in your neighborhood?

16. Do you work happily with others and do your part, even when the group is doing something you do not particularly enjoy?

17. Can you usually see the funny side of things, even when the joke is on you?

18. Do you like most of the girls in your group?

19. Do you enjoy doing things for others whether you get credit for them or not?

20. Do you like to help plan things for your group to do?

21. Does it make you happy to compliment others on the things they do well?

22. Do you remember the likeable qualities of your friends, and forget the things you dislike?

At a group meeting . . . Play Charming: Each girl draws two of the above numbers, from 1 to 22. Act them out. The rest of the group guess what point you're making.

Become a Charming Young Hostess

Being thoughtful of others and making everyone feel at home in your home is being a gracious hostess. This way, it's much more pleasant for the hostess and the guest.

Becoming Charming with Practice

At a group meeting . . . get ready for a party your group is planning! Plan what decorations you'll have. Practice setting the table and serving whatever food and beverage you will be having. Also learn, and try out, how to introduce guests. Then you'll be prepared on the big day!

At other group meetings . . . practice setting the table for different kinds of parties: a buffet, a tea, a luncheon or a dinner. Also, it will be fun to divide into small groups and think of things you would say and do to show you are thinking of others and helping them feel at home. Now act these out for the entire group! At another meeting, wouldn't you like to learn to polish silver, copper, and brass? Each girl might bring a piece to work on. It will be a joy to see your object shine brightly. Yes, there are many skills to learn when you become a charming young hostess!

Becoming Charming with Manners

Good manners show that you like people.

At a group meeting . . . Get your manners out. Dust them off. Plan a Musty Manners meeting. Act out what you would do in the following situations:

— Marilyn Manners and Cathy Charming are good friends. They try to be friendly with everyone. Do you? How can you show it?

— Marilyn makes her phone calls to Cathy short. Do you know why? Show how she can do it.

— Cathy listens when other people are talking. She tries not to interrupt, ever.

— These two girls are polite to each other (they try to be most of the time) and to grownups too. When they talk with grownups they are especially polite.

— They find radio and television programs the rest of the family enjoy when they are together. Why? Which ones would your family enjoy? Would you like them also?

— Cathy tries to remember to put away her belongings when she's finished using them. Why is that a good idea? What happens if she doesn't?

— Do you remember to say "Please" and "Thank you"? Do you like to have people say these words to you? How does your voice sound when you say "Hello" and "Thank you"? Try it!

— Do you say, "I'm going to—" —or do you say, "May I please—?" (You finish the sentences and act this out.)

Be a Good Housekeeper
Start with your Room

A room can look like the persons who use it. What does your room look like? If you share it with a sister, share the work in keeping it attractive.

Is the floor clean and is the furniture dusted?

Is it neat?

Is your bed made?

Learn to Sew

You'll need to have needles, thread, a thimble, pins, scissors, and a tape measure when you sew. Start your own sewing box and decorate it yourself. Why not cover a box with paper and trim it with symbols for sewing things, or cover it with a piece of fabric.

At a group meeting . . . have a sewing bee. Bring needles, thread, thimble, scissors in a case and a piece of cloth. Learn the basic sew-

BASIC SEWING STITCHES

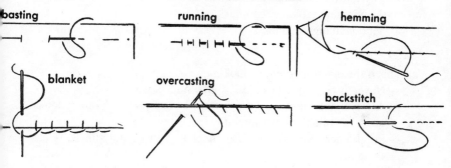

ing stitches. Some groups make samplers and show some of these stitches in colored embroidery thread. Others make samplers with the Law of the Camp Fire Girls embroidered in cross-stitch in color. Nice to frame and hang in your room.

Later you'll be able to make some of your own clothes. You can choose the cloth, colors and pattern. Your clothes can be a little different because you make them yourself. They cost less too.

Learn to Cook

Why don't you make friends with a cookbook? Look where the recipes for soups, meat and fish, vegetables, salads, and desserts are. Your mother or your guardian can help you choose and try something simple at first. Soon you'll be planning and preparing an entire menu.

Whenever you cook, you should do these things. We're sure you'll agree!

— Wear a clean apron over your dress.

— If your hair is long or fluffy, wear a ribbon or bandanna around it. Don't let it fly into the food, or your eyes, or near the flame.

— Never start to cook until you've washed your hands in warm soapy water. Dry them with a clean towel.

— Decide what you will cook. What would help mother most? What would the family like? Talk it over!

— Place the cookbook open at the recipe where you can read it easily.

— Now you are ready to begin: read the recipe carefully; ask questions if you are not sure.

— Lay out all utensils (pan, bowls, spoons, etc.) you will need on the kitchen table or counter.
— Set out all ingredients.

Safety in the Kitchen

This is the first ingredient in cooking.

— Never use the range unless a grownup is with you.
— Always close the oven door, quickly but gently. You or someone else might bump into it.
— Pot holders are handy. Use them to handle hot things. Wash them often.
— Is something out of reach? Don't stand on a chair; stand on a stool or a kitchen step stool that won't skid.
— Is something spilled? Be the first to wipe it clean. Someone might slip on it. Safety First!

Cooking Words . . . In those recipes you want to try, you're likely to meet a new set of words. You'll be told to baste, beat, cream, dice, dot, fold, garnish, grease, season, measure, and many more. Look in your mother's standard cookbook to find out what they mean, or in a cookbook for young people.

At a group meeting . . . your group might enjoy drawing from a hat the above words, and maybe others, too. At the next meeting, each girl could come ready to act out what her word means. They'll be easy to learn, but so important to know!

Plan an Attractive Meal

If it look delicious, it tastes even better, and it's more fun to serve. Here are points to consider as you plan your meal.

Make it healthy! Follow the Basic Four Guide:

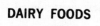

DAIRY FOODS

3 to 4 glasses milk including butter, cheese, ice cream, milk-made foods

MEAT GROUP

2 or more servings meats, fish, poultry, eggs or cheese or dry beans, peas, nuts

VEGETABLES AND FRUITS

4 or more servings dark green or yellow vegetables, citrus fruit or tomatoes

BREADS AND CEREALS

4 or more servings enriched or whole grain

Make it interesting! Have some soft, some chewy, some crunchy, and some crispy foods.

Make it tasty! Have different flavors, not all the same. For example, you wouldn't have tomato juice, tomato sauce and tomato salad in one meal, would you? Plan a variety of things that go together well. Look in a cookbook or magazine for ideas.

Make it attractive! Seek Beauty. Use foods of different colors to make the plate appealing to look at. If it's a lunch for day camp, or an outdoor meal for the family, wrap, pack and carry it so it will look just as tempting to eat.

Let's Market. You're going to shop for groceries? Then it's time to get ready.

1. Checking with the Basic Four foods, plan your menu and write it down.

2. Make a list of foods needed.

3. Check food on hand.

4. Write out a shopping list, and estimate how much you will spend. (If it's too much, you may have to start over at step 1.)

When you get home, you want to put your groceries away immediately.

1. Refrigerator items come first. The frozen foods go in the freezing section, while the meat, dairy products and some vegetables and fruits go in their proper places in the refrigerator.

2. Store canned goods and flour, sugar, etc., in cupboards.

3. Check the grocery bill. Does it compare with what you had planned to spend?

Set an Attractive Table. Setting your table carefully—just right— helps make your whole meal a great success!

Place knife, fork, spoons and the napkin so the ends are all in an even row at the bottom, about 1″ from the edge of the table. The glass goes right at the tip end of the knife. If adults have coffee or tea, the cup and saucer go at the right of the spoons.

The forks are always on the left of the plate. The knife and spoons are always on the right. The knife is always nearest the plate with the sharp edge towards the plate. For dinner, add a salad fork and a bread and butter plate which is placed above the forks.

Don't wait for a party to make your table look pretty. A Camp Fire Girl tries to make every meal a pretty meal for her family, with a few flowers, wild or from the garden, or a bowl of fruit or a small plant. Candles are fun for a special occasion evening meal.

Clean up the Kitchen. This doesn't sound like fun, does it? You can make it fun, if you sing while you work. Others will want to help you.

— Put food away. Left-overs in small containers. When they cool, cover and put them in the refrigerator.

— Learn the best way to wash dishes. Talk about this with your mother and your guardian. Will you air dry the dishes after scraping, rinsing, washing in hot water and rinsing again? Or will you use an electric dishwasher?

— Put utensils and dishes back in their places.

— Be sure the sink, the floor, the counters are left clean.

— Check to be sure gas and electricity are turned off.

Include Service

Is someone sick? Would you like to give someone a special treat, "just because"? Why not prepare a breakfast tray for them? Try to add something a little special each time. Use a bright colored dish or two. Include a flower in a tiny glass or a gay card of greeting just from you. It will be a lovely way to start the day.

"Take-a-Tea" is a wonderful idea for your group to do. Perhaps the person is unable to get out, or is new to your community. Or maybe you want to say "thank you" to a friend.

When your group takes a tea, you take all the refreshments, supplies, and equipment you will need. This would include paper napkins, a table centerpiece, favors, food, utensils. No doubt you will want to sing a few songs for your guest-in-her-own-home. Tell her about your group and ask her about herself.

CHAPTER 13

THE OUTDOORS

Have you ever packed your own picnic lunch to eat outdoors? Or made a trail lunch to take on a hike? Would you like to build a small fire and help cook a one-pot meal?

Have you ever dreamed of sitting around a campfire with your group, toasting marshmallows over the coals watching the fire glow?

To be a real camper you must know how to look after yourself and others out of doors. You'll discover all kinds of surprising things about nature too—plants, animals, birds, weather, and stars.

This chapter tells you how to be at home in the outdoors—first, with hikes and trail lunches; then on day trips with easy outdoor cooking. A back yard overnight is a thrill when you plan it carefully with your group and guardian. After many good cookouts and close-to-home overnights, your group will be ready to plan an overnight farther away.

It's a dream of almost every Camp Fire Girl to go to a Camp Fire Girls camp in the summer. There you have swimming, boating, dramatics, music, crafts, and all kinds of outdoor things! There are day camps and resident camps especially for Camp Fire Girls. Ask your guardian to get a camp folder.

Fun and Easy Outdoor Meetings

Try these once, twice, many times. The outdoors is a perfect place to do so many things!

· Take the business meeting out of doors on a porch, in a yard or neighborhood park.

· Go on a 6- to 10-block neighborhood hike. Look at tree shapes for one block, different kinds of flowers in yards the next; listen for birds in the next. . . .

· Go outdoors even when the weather isn't perfect. Have some active games or nature games.

· On a bright sunny day, postpone "indoor" plans until next week. Take an afternoon hike. Collect nature materials: pebbles, twigs, cones, leaves, cornhusks, reeds or weeds. Use them in nature crafts.

· On a hike in the country, *stop, look* and *listen* for interesting things

you'll discover in nature: growing things, clouds, nuts, rocks, birds and their nests, colors, snowflakes. Sometimes you'll discover tracks of animals or birds or people, in the sand or snow or mud. Have you seen cobwebs on the grass or the snow sparkling on a church steeple in the sun?

· On a city hike, discover different kinds of wood and rock used in buildings. Watch for ways in which man-made and nature-made things exist side by side. There's beauty in this connection. See how a street light makes patterns of leaf shadows! And there are so many sounds! Birds sing, wind whistles, leaves rustle, even in the city.

· Souvenirs? You might find some things you can take home with you to show at your next meeting. Remember to *protect* nature, not destroy it.

· Have a nature treasure hunt for things like 3 white pebbles, a bird feather, a bit of moss, 3 dead twigs that look like people or animals, 10 grasses or reeds, 2 dried weeds or milkweed cotton. Lay your treasures safely in a box for use at next week's meeting.

· Make little outdoor scenes with your treasure hunt finds. Arrange them on cardboard, the inside of the top of an empty egg carton, inside a box cover, on plaster of Paris, or on a smooth piece of wood. Add a bit of color with crayons. Plan what you'll do with your scenes. Will you exhibit them, give them to a shut-in, take them home for the family to see?

- Have a marshmallow munch. That's a hike with a marshmallow roast at the end, or back at the starting point (your meeting place).
- Have a group outdoor ceremonial in a lovely spot. Watch a sunset or a sunrise. Have breakfast afterwards if it's early.
- See-Feel-Hear Hike. Take paper and crayons and cardboard drawing boards. Sketch the colors you see. Compare the feel of stones, the texture of barks of trees, bushes, weeds, grasses. Listen to sounds of nature and man. Sit or stand quietly. Close your eyes. How many different sounds can you hear in two minutes?
- Nature Designs Hike. Watch for shapes of leaves, shapes of trees and bushes, shapes of stones. Look for designs in flower patterns, feathers, bird's wings, clouds. Take paper, pencil, and cardboard drawing board. Sketch the shapes you discover.
- Shades of Yellow Hike. Find one specimen of different leaves, bark, blossoms, stones, grasses, weeds, or feathers—anything—in any shade of yellow, green or orange. (Or do the same with reds and purples.) On a large plain color cardboard, arrange the specimens artistically from greens to yellows to orange. Fasten with Scotch tape. The effect of the lovely colors will amaze you!
- Here's a Dad-Daughter Treasure Hunt that's different! Each girl buries a special little treasure for her father. She marks the trail or makes symbols or leaf shapes to send him to the spot where it is hidden. The treasure hunt ends with a picnic lunch or cookout which the dads may help to prepare. Songs around a fire are nice too.
- Wintertime hikes and cookouts are wonderful fun! All the world looks so different. How lucky to be out when the sun is sparkling on new snow, or when everything is so quiet and the snowflakes are drifting down! Where do the tracks lead? What kind are they? What story do they tell? Plan winter fun during the holidays or on weekends.

Planning for a Hike or Other Outdoor Meeting

Make good plans. Everyone will have a better time if you talk these things over with your group and your guardian.

Decide Before You Go

1. Where and when will you go? Paths and trails through the woods, along the shore, or in a park are fun. Will you need to go by car, bus, or bike to where you can start to hike?

2. Why are you going? Just for fun? To practice your cooking skill? To enjoy nature, or all three?

3. What will you wear? Why should you wear oxfords or comfortable low heeled shoes and not sneakers? Should you take a coat or sweater? What will you need for wet weather? For snow? For very hot sun?

4. What about safety? Read "Safety Tips for Hikers" which follow. Why are these wise rules? Add others to them which should apply to your group.

5. Manners? Do you need permission to go where you've chosen? Or build a fire there? If so, your guardian gets this permission. Obey "No Trespassing" signs. What can you do to leave a clean trail and to help "Keep America Beautiful"? Check the "Good Outdoor Manners" section of this chapter.

6. What will you eat? Will it be a trailside lunch you packed at home, or something to cook out?

7. What equipment will you need to have with you?

    Your lunch? _____   Parent's permission slip? _____
    Sit-upon? _____   Rainy day equipment? _____
    Carfare? _____   Cup and eating utensils? _____
    Camera? _____   Book about birds, trees,
    or flowers? _____

8. How will you carry your equipment? It's best to leave your arms and hands free while you hike. Carry your things over your shoulder, around your waist, or gypsy fashion in a colorful bandanna tied to a stick. A bandanna can also be a bag for your trip treasures or a hot dishholder when you cook. In packing your food, put heaviest items on the bottom, and take only things you will need and which pack well.

Discuss Afterwards

1. When you return, talk over the trip and the fun you had. What did you like best? What did you discover that you didn't know before? What did you see that you hadn't seen before? How can you make better plans next time?

2. Start making plans for your next hike. With this experience behind you, maybe you'd like to make more of your own equipment and try another kind of menu.

Safety Tips for Hikers

It is important to talk over and make your own safety rules for your group. Here are important safety rules:

1. Always keep together. (One adult hikes near the front of the group and the other near the rear.)

2. Walk in pairs or singly; don't run while hiking. Walk on the left or facing the traffic. Wear something white and carry a flashlight if you walk at twilight or after dark.

3. Take short rest periods often. Take a longer rest after lunch. Talk over the best way to relax. If the ground is dry, lie flat on your back (jacket and sit-upon under you), and prop your feet against a big rock or tree.

4. Do not tease animals, domestic or other.

5. Never ask or accept rides with strangers.

6. Drink water only when your guardian knows it is pure. Pick and eat only things you and your guardian absolutely know.

7. Learn to recognize and avoid poisonous plants like poison ivy, oak and sumac.

8. At first sign of electrical storm, seek shelter away from any large trees.

Building Fires

A good camper needs to know where and how to build a safe fire. Find out what the fire laws are in your town and state. Observe them! Tell others about them. If a fire permit is required for your fire, be sure to get it in advance.

It's important to know how to tend and extinguish a fire too. Here are ten Fire Safety Precautions that will help you to be a good camper.

Fire Safety Precautions

1. Build your fire in a safe place, on sand, rocks or gravel, or in a fireplace. If on ground, clear a 10-foot circle, and remove all leaves, grass and twigs right down to the bare earth. Stones around the edge are very good.

2. Make your woodpile at the edge of this circle.

3. Build small fires, just large enough for your needs.

4. Never light a fire when you are alone. Never leave a fire alone. Watch it constantly.

5. Do not build a fire outdoors if the wind is blowing hard.

6. *Never* use kerosene or gasoline on or near a fire. Too dangerous!

7. Before building a fire, have pails or #10 tin cans of water or sand at the fire site. Wet burlap, and shovels are good to have, too.

8. Have box of baking soda or salt near a cooking fire to use in case grease catches fire. *Never* use flour or water on grease.

9. Do not build a fire near a tree trunk, exposed roots or under low branches.

10. Put the fire out—*completely out*—when you no longer need it. Never leave a fire until you and your guardian are sure it is dead out. Spread the coals with rake or shovel. They will burn faster. Sprinkle water on them by hand. Do not throw pails of water on the fire; this causes smoke and steam.

Kinds of Wood for Fire Building

You'll need three sizes of wood: 1) tinder, 2) kindling, and 3) fire-wood. The tinder lights the kindling, which in turn ignites the bigger firewood which keeps the fire hot.

1. Tinder: This is your smallest wood—anything light and dry enough to be lighted by a match. Find wood not thicker than a match, but longer. Try tying little bundles of twigs together at one end. Stand like a tepee. You may use tiny dry twigs from evergreen trees, shavings, cedar and birchbark (from dead trees only), pine cones, dry milkweed floss, or little bundles of dry twigs from tops of bushes.

2. Kindling: Use softwood, from pencil-thick to thumb-thick size, about 8-10 inches long.

3. Firewood: This is what keeps your fire hot. It will make good coals if you use hardwood and have plenty of dry tinder and kindling. Use dry wood, from kindling size up to pieces as thick as your wrist and ankle. Use softwood for a hot fire for boiling, quick cooking and reflector oven baking. You will need to keep feeding a softwood fire. It burns out quickly.

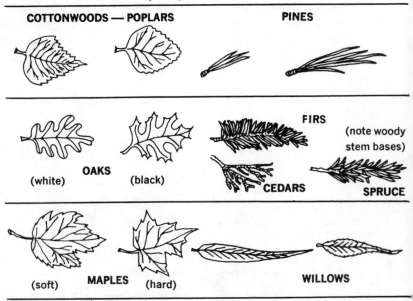

Use hardwoods for a long-burning fire and beds of coals. This is good for toasting, broiling, roasting and baking.

Which is softwood and which is hardwood? Softwood comes from trees like evergreens which have cones and needles, such as cedar, fir, hemlock, pine, spruce. It also comes from broadleafed trees like aspen, basswood, gray birch, cottonwood, willow, poplar. Hardwood trees grow slowly: apple, ash, beech, yellow birch, elm, hickory, maples, mesquite, oak, walnut. Hardwood feels heavier in your hand than softwood.

NOTE FOR FIRE BUILDERS: Use heavy canvas work gloves or pot holders when working with kettles and fire building. Put kettle on as soon as you start the fire! Saves wood and time.

Selecting and Gathering Wood

1. Dead wood burns best. Use green sticks only when fire is very hot. A dead twig will snap. A green one will bend.
2. Try to find dead branches on lower limbs of trees, the drier the better. Wood lying flat on the ground is apt to be damp.
3. Wood that crumbles is rotting. It is going back to vegetable matter, and it will not burn well. Don't use it to build fires.
4. Split wood burns better than round wood. It gives off more heat.
5. Driftwood burns well, and gives off colored flames. Nice for a campfire!

Making Your Woodpile

Sort your wood by size—tinder, kindling, firewood. Pile it neatly.

Have it far enough from your fire so sparks cannot reach it. If sharing a camp site, leave some wood for the next group.

Take Care with Matches

Use waterproof matches and carry them in metal container (a bouillon cube can is good). How do you make matches waterproof? There are two ways: apply colorless nail polish to the tips. That's the easiest way. Or dip the tips in paraffin, but do this with your guardian present. (Melt paraffin in a tin can set in hot water, like a double boiler. Never melt paraffin over a direct flame; never cover it; never leave it.)

The Tepee Fire

Now that you have cleared a fire circle, made a woodpile, have your waterproof matches and pail of water or sand for extinguishing ready —let's build the fire!

1. Start with a tepee (or wigwam) fire. That's the way you'll start all fires. Stand with the wind blowing against your back. Lay 3 (or 4) sticks of kindling in the center of your fire circle. Place so that there is space underneath for the wind to fan the fire.

2. Stand a bunch of tinder twigs (tepee style), or place a small pile of tinder in the center of the larger sticks. Leave a space to insert your match at the center and bottom of tinder.

3. Stand pieces of kindling on end around and against the tinder; smaller pieces first, then larger. Don't cover the opening you've left for your match to light the tinder! The fire burns upward. It needs plenty of air coming in from side or underneath. That's why the tepee shape is good.

   Tip for indoor fireplace fire: Use tepee to start fire, or use half a tepee against a log in indoor fireplace. Don't forget to leave space for draft.

4. To light the fire, kneel with your back to the wind. Strike the match away from you on a dry rough stone. Tip match head down. Cup hands around it. When burning well, stick it in the airspace in tinder. Leave it there. Blow gently at base of fire. Fire must have draft underneath.

5. When kindling is flaming briskly, add firewood—small sticks, then larger, one by one. Add wood slowly. Have each piece touching other pieces, tepee style.

Other Kinds of Fires

The tepee is your basic fire, a quick fire for broiling. Other kinds of fires can be built using this as a starter. Like these:

Crisscross Fire: Begin with a tepee fire. Around it lay in crisscross fashion, sticks about an inch thick (split logs are good), and an inch apart. Have some larger sticks on the bottom layers. Light the tepee in center. In a short time the crisscross wood falls to make a bed of nice coals.

Hunter-Trapper Fire: This is good when several dishes are to be cooked at the same time. Place two green logs side by side, closer together at one end. These support your kettle, pot or broiler. Build one or more tepee or crisscross fires between the logs. Stones may be used instead of logs. A damper stick is good to provide air when needed. This fire uses little wood and keeps fire in small area. Can provide good coals.

Trench Fire: This is similar to the one above. In a trench dug in the earth, lay tepee of tinder and kindling. Build crisscross over the top. The coals drop into the trench. Rest pans on green sticks or metal rods. You can rake coals to one end and build up tepee for quick cooking at the other end.

Reflector Fire: This is used for baking. See Sketch. *The Outdoor Book* tells how to build and use this fire.

The Cookout

If you are planning a hike with a cookout, or just a cookout, there are big and little jobs to be done to get that delicious meal ready.

Before you start you'll need shoppers and packers, and planners for the games, songs and honors that can be earned. Everyone can't do the same thing at the same time at the cookout, so divide up the jobs. This is a chance to Glorify Work, because cookout jobs are fun. Be Johnny-on-the-spot when it's your turn, and still have time to play games, look at the view, or write a poem between times!

Divide the jobs. Some groups draw names, some choose jobs, and some make a chart. Here's a sample Kaper Chart that can be tacked up on a tree:

KAPER CHART

Fire Builders and Tenders	Cooks	Table Setters and Servers	Dish Washers	Program Planners	Clean-up and Pack-up
Liz Judy	Cindy Sally	Carolyn Marilyn	Sue Ann	Mary Diane	Kathy Becky

Be sure each girl knows her job. It's a good idea for everyone to gather wood, first thing. The fire builders help too, then supervise making the woodpile. Don't collect a lot more wood than you need.

Have enough hikes and cookouts so that every girl can learn how to do all six kapers. Rotate so different girls work together.

Fire Builders Supervise making the woodpile. Take care of it. Keep it neat and away from sparks and flames. Build the fire and keep it burning. Find out whether quick heat or coals will be needed. Keep fire burning long enough to heat dishwater. Have fire extinguishing equipment (pails of water, sand) at the fire. Be responsible for putting out the fire when through.

Cooks Unpack the food and cooking utensils. Prepare, cook, and serve the food from cooking pans.

Table Setters As hostesses, arrange an attractive spot for the table and seating (even if on the ground). Choose a spot a little away from the fire and out of the smoke. Have a simple nature centerpiece, a bit of pine or fern for a place card perhaps, or tiny bouquets of wild flowers. (Know which flowers may be picked.) Lay out dishes and paper napkins. Select and lead Grace before the meal. Put the food on the table or assist the cooks when each girl is served at the fire.

Dish Washers No one says "I love that job!" but it can be fun when several help and songs go along with it! Make it easy. Rub soap or a paste of detergent on the outside of cooking kettles *before* they go on the fire. Soot comes off easily then. Have a kettle of hot water ready when the meal is over. Put cooking dishes to soak in cold water while you eat. Scrape, wipe with paper, rinse dishes before and after washing. Sometimes each girl washes her own dishes, and the dish washers just do the cooking dishes.

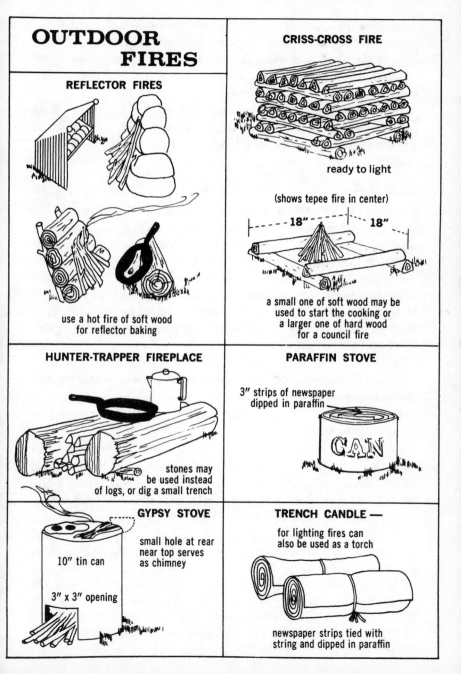

OUTDOOR FIRES

REFLECTOR FIRES

use a hot fire of soft wood
for reflector baking

CRISS-CROSS FIRE

ready to light

(shows tepee fire in center)

18"   18"

a small one of soft wood may be
used to start the cooking or
a larger one of hard wood
for a council fire

HUNTER-TRAPPER FIREPLACE

stones may
be used instead
of logs, or dig a small trench

PARAFFIN STOVE

3" strips of newspaper
dipped in paraffin

CAN

GYPSY STOVE

small hole at rear
near top serves
as chimney

10" tin can

3" x 3" opening

TRENCH CANDLE —

for lighting fires can
also be used as a torch

newspaper strips tied with
string and dipped in paraffin

Program Planners Plan time for the group to look around . . .
see the colors, the sun sparkling on the waters, the clouds drifting by
or perhaps watch a brilliant sunset reflected in a lake, or on house
windows. Have a few songs, a game or two, and always time to earn
some special Outdoors Craft honors.

Clean-up and Pack-up Everyone helps on this, but two or three
should be in charge to see that nothing is left behind, nothing is lost,
and equipment is well packed. Leave the camp site neater than you
found it.

Kinds of Meals

Let's go on a picnic hike! Let's cook supper on a gypsy stove!

A Trail Lunch: Prepare a trail lunch for that short hike, when you don't
want to cook out. You can do this either at home or in the group meeting before the hike. Vary it as you wish. Add your own ideas but include
the "Basic Four." Try using two kinds of bread in one sandwich, one
white enriched bread and one dark bread. Butter both slices to keep
filling from soaking into the bread. Wrap in waxed paper or foil. Foil-
lined ice cream bags are good for carrying fruit or sandwiches. A trail
lunch needs to be light.

What is a trail lunch? Sandwiches, raw vegetable, dried or fresh
fruit; and for dessert, nuts, chocolate bars, cookie. Have milk if possible
and available at site.

For the next hike, have a lunch prepared at home *and* something
cooked on the hike.

One-pot Meals: Most of these require a fire with flames but watch that
you don't have scorched food! One-pot meals are not just meat and
vegetables thrown together. They too must have the "Basic Four" foods,
so add a salad or carrot and celery sticks, milk or cocoa. Fruit is tasty
for dessert. Recipes can be found in *The Outdoor Book*.

Stick Cookery: Another way to cook outdoors is to toast or broil.
Choose a green branch about 30″ long and about as thick as your index
finger. Willow is good. (Do not use rhododendron, laurel, poison oak
or poison sumac.) Save your stick. It can be used several times. If you
cannot find a green stick, wrap 8-10″ of the pointed end of a dry stick
with aluminum foil. For bread sticks, use a stick twice as big around as
your thumb. Scrape off bark at cooking end; grease before winding
dough around it. Leave space between winds.

Aluminum Foil Cookery: Would you like to have a perfect meal outdoors with no kettles to carry and no dishes to wash? Try it with aluminum foil. Foil can be used as a pressure cooker to cook meat, vegetables, biscuits or desserts. Use it to make your own kettle or frying pan.
Utensils: Fold double foil over a coha toaster to form a rim and handle.
Fold up the edges and make a pan. Use heavy duty foil or double thick-
ness of regular foil.

What is a coha? Use a wire coat hanger (co-ha) to make this toaster
or broiler. Cut coat hanger with wire cutting pliers. (Ordinary pliers
won't work.) Straighten ends with hammer. Bend to desired shape and
hammer again to help keep shape.

The fire is an important part of aluminum foil cooking. A bed of hot
coals is just right. Cooking time varies with food. At first you may need
to open your package carefully, to check on the cooking.

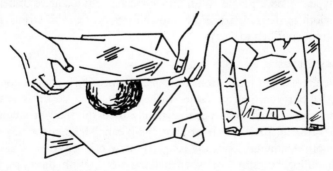

The food should be placed on a piece of foil large enough to fold all
open edges over three times. Allow room for hamburgers or biscuits
to expand while cooking. Add at least 1 or 2 tbsp. of water or butter to
meats or vegetables before wrapping, to prevent scorching. Avoid
puncturing the package before cooking.

Place package directly on coals. Turn when half done. To test, pull package from fire with tongs and unfold edges. Refold and return to coals if not done. Soon you'll know about how long it takes to cook your favorite food. Eat directly from the foil and save dishes!

Make Your Own Equipment

Bandanna Kit Use a bandanna kerchief or better still, make your own from a piece of cloth about 24″ square. Decorate it with symbols, or tie-dye it. Tie opposite corners with a square knot (with your lunch or treasures in the center, of course!). There you are with a gypsy kit to carry on a stick over your shoulder, or to tie on your belt.

Easy Kit For trip treasures or lunch: Make this hike kit from a mesh bag. Fruits and vegetables often come in these bags. Save one and make yourself a hike kit, like this: Use a large yarn needle and a double thread of heavy cotton rug yarn or similar material. Start at the bottom, weaving in and out across warp and weft. Go 'round and 'round the bag, knotting the yarn with a square knot each time you rethread your needle. Be careful not to weave through to the other side of the bag. *The Outdoor Book* shows you how to make other kits.

Sit-upons To be used as a cushion when ground is damp or cold. These may be simple or fancy, permanent or for "one sitting." Here is one type, called a pinkie. With pinking shears cut a square of heavy plastic cloth in desired size. Fold and roll tightly, tie with string, and dangle from your belt to carry.

Gypsy Stoves

These are easy to make from tin cans. Younger girls should not try this. Ask your guardian or father to help you, because tin is sharp. Use only cans which have been originally used for food products— a clean #10 can, or a cookie or shortening can. Make edges of open end smooth. Hammer down any rough spots. Wear heavy work gloves when handling hot stove or when making stove. With tin snips, cut a 3″ square door. With a beverage can opener, punch chimney holes in the opposite side. To use: Put your stove on the cleared ground. Tie a small bunch of smallest twigs at one end. Stand tepee style to make tepee fire. When this is burning well, place the stove over the fire so the opening faces the wind. Because the wood is so small you'll need to feed the fire constantly. Two girls work together.

Fry or pan broil directly on the tin surface, but burn off the lacquer first. Heat the top. Remove from fire, using work gloves. Grease and wipe off. Then add a little fat again and cook.

Gypsy stoves may also be used with paraffin burners instead of wood. For full directions on how to make these, see Chapter 14 in *The Outdoor Book*.

Good Outdoor Manners

With all the fun of outdoor cooking and trips, Camp Fire Girls are thoughtful of the next hiker or camper and the owner of the property. Let's be sure to observe good conservation ways. Many states have laws about picking wild flowers. What are the laws in your state? The Audubon Junior Programs give us this good advice:

"Pick, if you must, one flower face, if *nine* more blooms
    are left in place,

Two feet square must hold that many; otherwise *look*—but
    don't pick *any!*"

Conservation

Conservation means care and protection, to keep things in a safe and sound condition.

If you conserve your favorite books or your bicycle, you put them away carefully when you have finished with them.

To conserve flowers, you watch them grow; you water and weed the flower garden. You save wild flowers by finding them, learning to know them, but *not* by picking them! Leave them for others to love.

How can you help to conserve our natural resources, such as our forests, lakes and streams, soil, flowers, birds and animals? We need to protect all of these. What can you and your group do to help?

At a group meeting . . . why not plan a ceremonial about conservation? Tell someone about the conservation pledge. Or have a window exhibit for Camp Fire's birthday week, using conservation as a theme. The *Conservation* book (Cat. No. D-249) will give your guardian ideas. Camp Fire Girls can Seek Beauty, Pursue Knowledge, and Give Service through conservation!

CONSERVATION PLEDGE

I give my pledge as an American to save and faithfully to defend from waste the natural resources of my country—its soil and minerals, its forests, waters and wildlife.

Collecting Leaves and Ferns

A collection of leaves, weeds and grasses is fun to make. Girls and boys in Hawaii make a collecting press and mount their leaves this way. Have nature specimens fresh. They must dry quickly. To make a simple press, knock off two sides of orange crate or wooden box. (If specimens are small, use the two ends instead.) Make a filler for the inside from layers of newspaper or blotting paper. Place specimens in the center. Use luggage strap or rope to hold it together firmly.

Mounting the specimens: To mount pressed leaves or other plants, mix glue with one part vinegar and smear rather thickly over a piece of glass. Lay the dried specimen on the glass and press down gently until back is covered with glue. Now transfer to paper, cover with paper and again press gently with your hand, so the whole surface is glued. This method does not need a paste brush which breaks the leaf when it is dry.

Now for That Camping Trip

When you have begun to feel at home in the out-of-doors on hikes and treasure hunts, you will want to have a real camping trip. This is quite different from planning a party at home. It takes even more careful thought ahead of time. Camping outdoors requires consideration for other people and respect for their property.

If you are a Wood Gatherer, or if you've been to camp for one or two summers, you are probably ready for an overnight trip. If this is your first experience in camping and living outdoors, you'll need to catch up on fire building and outdoor cooking by earning some Outdoors Craft honors first. This will be fun too. A nice back yard often provides just the spot for a first cookout or overnight trip, and plenty of time to cook a tempting meal. Appetites are always good outdoors.

An overnight camping trip gives you a chance to learn how to take care of yourself outdoors and cook your meals over an outdoor fire. You are a responsible member of the "team." Because at least three meals are cooked outdoors, you can try out new recipes. Try one-pot meals, or cooking without utensils (have you ever made bread twists on a stick, and filled them with jam?), quick pizzas and other yummy recipes.

Try to have a pre-trip mothers' meeting, and let them in on your plans. They'll be excited too! Tell them where you are going, what time you will return. Tell them about your plans for transportation, the cost, and about their written permission which you need in order to go on the trip. Share all of your plans with them.

Two one-day camping trips can be just as much fun and you can cook the same luscious foods outdoors. The two trips, taken on separate days, spread your camping fun over a longer period. There is always the overnight trip to look forward to later.

Choose the two one-day trips if you have not had much camping experience, or if your group has not yet found a really suitable spot for overnight camping.

CHAPTER 14

GOOD CITIZENSHIP

Citizenship in the United States of American is a wonderful privilege. It is also a great responsibility for each of us. *Everybody* counts. Everyone has rights which must be respected, and responsibilities to live up to. This is true for young citizens like you, as well as for adult citizens.

While you are growing up, you will learn to be a good citizen in a democracy. You work and play with others who are both different from you and like you. You respect them. You are willing to listen to their ideas, whether they are personal friends or acquaintances. Also, your Camp Fire group is a democracy. You and the other members of the group decide *together* what your group activities will be and how they are to be carried out.

Learning Citizenship in Camp Fire through Honors

Camp Fire Girls suggests many ways to practice good citizenship. One is to earn honors in Citizenship Craft. Try some—or all of them! They're fun.

Learning Citizenship in Camp Fire in Group Meetings

Group meetings provide more ways. Here are some ideas:

- *"Citizenship is a wonderful privilege."* This could be a theme for a group ceremonial, or for a meeting planned around a patriotic holiday. Perhaps you will decide to include *The American's Creed*. This was written by William Tyler Page in 1918 during a nationwide contest on this subject. That's eight years after Camp Fire Girls was founded!

- *Become better acquainted with our Bill of Rights!* It assures the freedom of everyone and is a part of the Constitution of the United States. Bring a copy of it to a group meeting. With the girls and your guardian, talk about what the Bill of Rights means to you and to every other citizen of the United States. Now divide into groups, and each try to act out the meaning of some of these rights. You might play Bill of Rights charades. Or, illustrate the various parts of the Bill of Rights by using magazines, newspapers, photographs, and pictures you draw or paint yourself. This would be good for a citizenship or a Camp Fire Girls display, or as a gift to other children to help them learn more about the Bill of Rights.

- *Have a "My Town—Then and Now" Day.* Who were the people who settled your area? Why did they come? What did the town look like then? How did they live? Now consider your town today. How does its government operate? What services does it provide? Who works for the town and how are they selected? What other services are provided to people in your town today? What does the library, the newspaper, the museum do for the town?

How do you find out all of these things? That's half the fun! To find out about your town long ago, talk to people who know about the history of your community. Visit local historical sites, museums, libraries, to trace down the past. Maybe some of the older citizens of your community can fill you in on some of the history, from first-hand experience.

To find out about your town *now,* here are some suggestions:

Visit public buildings. These might be institutions, museums, libraries, police and fire departments. Ask city officials to tell about their duties and the services they perform. Your guardian makes arrangements ahead of time, for all these trips.

Interview a government official. He might be from the city, the county, or the state. Ask him to explain to you the differences between these three levels of government. Perhaps one of the dads among your group works in government.

Invite a representative. Ask someone from your city or county health department to tell the group about health laws that protect children.

Visit a voting precinct headquarters. With your guardian, make such a visit at election time, to find out what happens on voting day.

Attend a naturalization ceremony, if you have the chance. This is when new residents in your town are making their promise to be loyal citizens of the United States. You might give them a special red, white, and blue nosegay (for the ladies) or a buttonhole flower (for the men).

Tour a local newspaper. Ask one of the editors how the newspaper helps your town.

What will you do with all of your information? Why not write a play or plan a ceremonial using some of it? Your parents, grandparents, and friends would probably love to be your guests.

Learn about the Flag of the United States of America

Our country's flag stands for all the traditions and hopes of the United States of America. It is a symbol of strength and courage, of sacrifice and loyalty, and of national unity. It is also a symbol of our democratic ideals. Because of this, every good citizen loves and respects it. To show proper respect, you will need to know:

The Pledge of Allegiance to the Flag of the United States of America

"I pledge allegiance to the flag of the United States of America and to the Republic for which it stands, one Nation under God, indivisible, with liberty and justice for all."

Here are two other statements which well express American ideals:

The American's Creed

"I believe in the United States of America as a Government of the people, by the people, for the people; whose just powers are derived from the consent of the governed; a democracy in a republic, a sovereign Nation of many sovereign States; a perfect union, one and inseparable, established upon those principles of freedom, equality, justice, and humanity for which American patriots sacrificed their lives and fortunes.

"I therefore believe it is my duty to my country to love it; to support its constitution; to obey its laws; to respect its flag; and to defend it against all enemies."   William Tyler Page.

The Freedom Pledge

"I am an American. A free American.
Free to speak, without fear
Free to worship God in my own way
Free to stand for what I think right
Free to oppose what I believe wrong
Free to choose those who govern my country.
This heritage of Freedom I pledge to uphold
For myself and all mankind."

The American Heritage Foundation.

General Rules of Good Flag Etiquette

1. Show pride in your flag by standing straight and tall, facing the flag during a flag ceremony. Salute by placing your right hand over your heart. This is correct whether you are in Camp Fire Girls costume or not. It is the citizen's salute.

2. The flag should be flown outdoors from sunrise to sunset, whenever good weather permits.

3. The blue field of stars is at the top. If the flag is hung flat, the blue field is at the top left as you face it.

4. The flag of the United States should never touch the ground, never be used as part of a costume or decoration, never have another flag or decoration above it.

5. The flag of the United States should be kept clean and mended. When it is old and worn out, the flag should be destroyed, preferably by burning, and always with respect.

How to Participate in a Flag Ceremony

Flag ceremonies show our reverence and appreciation for what our flag stands for. It is, therefore, an honor for Camp Fire Girls and all U.S. citizens to participate in such a ceremony. Camp Fire Girls respectfully take part in these flag ceremonies and do everything they can to make them dignified and beautiful.

General Rules and Customs of Flag Ceremonies

FLAGS CARRIED

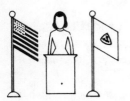

ON A PLATFORM

1. When in procession with another flag, the national flag is on the marching right.

2. When in procession with a line of other flags, the national flag is in front of the center of the line.

3. When displayed from a staff on a speaker's platform or stage, the national flag is placed to the *speaker's* right. Other flags are to the left.

4. When displayed where there is *not* a platform or a stage, the national flag should be placed to the *audience's* right, with other flags to the left of the audience.

5. When the flags of two or more nations are displayed together, they should be of equal size, and flown from separate staffs of equal height. International usage forbids the display of the flag of one nation above that of another in time of peace.

6. When displayed in a group of state or organizational flags, the national flag should be at the center and at the highest point.

Procedure for Camp Fire Girls Flag Ceremonies

There is no set procedure for civilian flag ceremonies, and no special one for Camp Fire Girls. The key to planning a successful flag ceremony is to remember that it should always be done with dignity, respect, and beauty. And it should be brief.

Girls who participate in a flag ceremony as members of Camp Fire Girls wear service costumes and present a clean, well groomed appearance. The color guards, and perhaps the entire group, may choose to wear white gloves. Posture should be perfect and every movement purposeful.

The outline which follows is only a *sample* of ideas which groups might include. You may wish to consider them when planning with your group. Have the kind of flag ceremony which is most suitable for you.

Flag ceremonies are performed by color guards. These include one flag bearer and at least one other color guard for each flag.

Sample Flag Ceremony

Attention: Audience stands at attention and salutes for entrance of the flag. A color guard may say, "Please stand and salute for the presentation of the colors." (Remember, the civilian salute is hand over heart. Civilians then show full attention by standing with hands at sides, men removing their hats.)

Entry of the Flag: A color guard may say, "Color Guard, advance," or a bugle call "Advance" may be sounded. The U.S. flag is in front or to the right. Each flag is carried by a flag bearer and is flanked by or followed by one or two other color guards. The flag bearer holds the flag staff before her, vertical, or slanted slightly forward. The left hand is near the bottom of the staff; the right hand is placed about a foot or two above.

Usually the entrance is most effective if the flag or flags come from the back of the audience, by either a center aisle or the side aisles. Other participants follow the color guards.

Flag to flag stands: When the stands are on a platform or on a stage, the U.S. flag is carried to the stand which is to the right of the speaker. At the same time, the Camp Fire Girls or other flag is carried to the stand to the speaker's left. *When there is no stage or platform,* the U.S. flag is carried to the stand which is to the right of the audience. At the same time the Camp Fire Girls flag is carried to the stand to the left of the audience.

Placement of flags: A color guard may say: "Place colors," or "Place flags." A color guard kneels to help each flag bearer guide the staff into the stand, then rises and steps back to position. All face national flag.

Pledge of Allegiance: As soon as the flags are in place, the Pledge of Allegience is said. One of the participants leads this. Everyone except the color guard salutes the flag and says the Pledge. The color guard simply stands at attention throughout the ceremony. Unless the national anthem is to follow, the audience and girls then remove hands from hearts but remain at attention.

Song: The group may choose to lead a stanza of a patriotic song. Besides "The Star Spangled Banner," other suitable songs are "America," "God Bless America," and "America the Beautiful." If the national anthem is used, all remain in salute position until it is ended.

Poem: A patriotic poem or thought may be given here instead of, or in addition to, the patriotic song. This may be original or not, done as choral speaking or by single girls. Remember, though, that the flag ceremony should be *brief;* everyone is still standing at attention.

Other: "The Camp Fire Girls Law" or "Wohelo Cheer" may be sung.

End of flag ceremony: A color guard may say: "Color Guards retreat." Color guards turn and leave. Group leaves with the same order and good posture with which they entered. Other participants follow in orderly procession.

Retreat of colors: This occurs after a program or after a longer flag ceremony such as one which might be held on Independence Day. Color guards remove the flags from their stands and carry them out in procession. The rest of the group follows. A bugle call "Retreat" may be sounded. The audience stands at attention until the flag has left the room.

How to Fold the Flag

There is a definite procedure for folding the national flag.

1. Fold the flag in thirds lengthwise, with the blue field on the outside. If it is a large flag, fold it in halves and then in quarters.

2. While one girl holds the blue field with two hands, another girl makes a triangular fold at the opposite end. Additional color guards may hold out their hands to form a table on which the flag may be folded.

3. Continue to fold in triangles while the first girl holds the flag tight. When it is completely folded into one triangle, only the blue field will show.

References on the U.S. Flag and Flag Ceremonies

Public Law #829—77th Congress (Chapter 806—20th Session).
Our Flag—DOD Pamphlet 5-62. For sale by the Superintendent of Documents, U.S. Government Printing Office, Washington, D. C. 20025.
Let's Be Right on Flag Etiquette—distributed by National Americanism Commission, the American Legion, Indianapolis, Indiana, 46206.

Learning Citizenship in Camp Fire through Service

Have a Festival of Giving. In your town may be some or all of the following:

children's hospitals	day nurseries
crippled children's hospitals	children's institutions
mental hospitals	institutions for mentally retarded

speech therapy and other clinics for children

They all can use many things which those who are being cared for will enjoy. Check first, to see whether you might make

stuffed animals and dolls	beanbags
jewelry boxes	scrapbooks
bags of building blocks	see-and-feel books
washcloth bath mitts, slippers	puppet kits
mobiles and favors for special holidays	surprise balls

You may find there are other things you can make which they would rather have.

Be Johnnies on the Spot. Camp Fire Girls in many places count, sort and stack material for the campaign kits of the United Fund or Community Chest. In this way and others, the girls show their appreciation for the community funds which support the Camp Fire Girls program.

"Adopt" Someone Special. Camp Fire groups often "adopt" a girl who is ill. They take her games, toys, storybooks. They share each group meeting with her through a letter or by sending special refreshments. Sometimes she too becomes a registered member of Camp Fire Girls!

Other groups have adopted older friends. All-year-round gifts, running errands, writing letters, friendly visits mean much to elderly people.

Share with Others. Collect books, magazines, and good comic books for lending libraries at day nurseries, play centers for children, children's institutions and hospitals, and migrant camps.

Help Others. Ask the Fire Department, Salvation Army or another organization if you can help in their Christmas toy salvage and repair work. Take part in your city safety campaign.

"Get Out the Vote." Discuss in your group why it is important for adults to vote. Help in your neighborhood to distribute literature reminding people to register for voting. On election day, remind your parents and neighbors by asking them, "Have you voted today?"

Protect Wildlife. Living creatures need you. They need homes and food, among other things, and you can help. Find out what birds and other wild creatures eat. Birds love berries, probably as much as you like an ice cream cone. Could you plant a berry bush for them? Ask forest preserve or park officials about how many and what kinds, and where you may plant. Suet, peanut butter, and seeds are tasty treats for birds during the winter. Providing these is another way of being a good citizen. Would you like to make a birdhouse? Making houses for bluebirds was an annual project several years ago—and it's still a good idea.

Give a Welcome! Is there someone new in your school or in your neighborhood? New places can seem very strange. When have you ever been in a new situation and felt that way? But there's an easy cure. Smile! Show the newcomer around and help him or her get acquainted. Maybe she's a girl about your age and would like to join your Camp Fire group. Ask her to do other things with you too.

Do National Projects. Keep America Beautiful, Project Share, Pen Friends, Needlework Guild, Edith M. Kempthorne Fund, all are national service projects. They help you be a good citizen, too. Find in Chapter 19 how you can take part in them. It is fun to know that Camp Fire Girls all across the nation are doing them, too—and you may earn a special honor for completing each.

THE LIVELY ARTS

These are the creative arts. Do you like to sing, and make music? Dance? Act out stories? Create something of your own with your hands and heart? This chapter tells some ways you can do this.

The Sound of Music

Make your own instruments, and learn to accompany your songs and music. Try the songs in Chapter 11, and in the book *Music Makers*.

Drum: A large coffee or potato chip can, or a sturdy round carton with one or both ends removed, will make a fine frame for your drum. Or you can use a wooden salad bowl. Decorate your drum frame with symbols or other designs.

For the drum head, stretch a layer of heavy paper over the open end of the frame, *and* a layer of cheesecloth or muslin over the paper. Tack or tie these tightly to the drum frame, so that the drum head is taut. Moisten the drum head slightly. When it is dry, spray or brush on two or more coats of shellac. And there you are!

Now for drumsticks. Pad end of two sticks with cotton. Stretch and tie muslin over the cotton. You're a drummer!

Tambourine: Around the rim of a heavy paper or tin plate, pierce six evenly spaced holes. Decorate with symbols or other designs.

From 18 metal bottle caps, take out the cork liners, and pierce holes in the caps with a large nail. (Be careful.) Cut six 8-inch pieces of cord, and thread each cord through three bottle caps, tying a knot between caps. Tie caps to holes in plate, and you have your own tambourine.

Human-A-Phone: Make a large curtain, about 10 feet wide and 8 feet high. Use old sheets, unbleached muslin, or large sheets of paper stapled or taped together. Paint a large clef on it and the eight notes of the musical scale. The notes must be large enough to be cut out for a girl's head to poke through. Hang the curtain, and let some of the group poke their heads through, as human "notes." With a girl as the conductor, you are ready to sing. Each girl will sing the words which fall on her note. Now try harmonies.

Dramatics

How many times have you heard "Act it out"? And how many times have you thought that it would be fun, for the moment, to become somebody else? Here are some of the many ways you can do this.

Play: This is a story which actors and actresses tell by acting and speaking as if they were the people in the story. Often the players wear costumes and use properties—a table, a tablecloth, chairs, a vase of flowers—to help the audience understand the story.

Write your own play, or find one that suits the occasion. Use ideas for plays from Camp Fire Girls lore, from literature, history, or current events.

Monologue: One person alone acts out a situation, and speaks as though she is talking with others. The trick is to be able to tell enough, by one person's conversation and actions, so that an audience will be entertained learning what is happening. Try doing a monologue by talking into a telephone.

Pantomime: This is acting out a situation or story, by using parts of the body—your face, and hands, etc.—but not your voice.

Can you pantomime eating corn on the cob, picking flowers and arranging them, trying on hats, walking in the rain? Don't make this just a guessing game like charades. Plan a complete scene. After you have finished, ask your audience how successful you were.

Choral Speaking: This is having a group speaking poetry or dramatic pieces as a chorus. You put special emphasis on the sound and meaning of what you are speaking together, much as a good singing group does. In group singing, there are high voices which are sopranos, and lower voices which are altos. For choral speaking, you can group people's voices in much the same way. Another way you can encourage a dramatic effect is to have several lines spoken by a solo voice or a small group. It's fun to experiment with many different ways before deciding which way is best.

Consider, also, how best to get across to the audience the meaning of the words you are speaking. Can you imagine how differently you might speak "running softly through the woods" and "Clang! Clang! warned the fire engine, as it screeched around the corner."

How do you sound as a group? Can your words be understood? Is one part too loud? Too fast? Perhaps you'll need to work on speaking more clearly. Maybe changing the position of one or two girls will help the chorus sound more balanced. Try choral speaking using the Desire of the rank you are achieving.

Stagecraft

Not everyone wants to be an actress, and there are many exciting ways to be a part of the theater without being "on stage." You can learn about costumes, make-up, and lighting. You can plan and make scenery, or help supply the sound effects, or the music. You can make a poster to advertise the show. Or you can prompt the actors from behind the scenes.

Shadow Pictures: These are scenes acted out behind screens. Put up a sheet or screen across a doorway or the front of a stage. Place a bright light on the floor a few feet behind the sheet. The actors stand between the two, but closer to the screen. They try to keep their bodies in profile and very close to the screen for the best effect. The light may be moved around to get the best shadow. Now practice acting out a story, using any props needed. Present it for a group of Blue Birds. Little Red Riding Hood, anyone?

Scroll Show: Mark off a roll of shelf paper, wrapping paper, or the wrong side of wall paper so that each girl has a big drawing space. Old sheets stitched together may also be used. On this scroll, draw scenes to tell a story, using crayons or paints very boldly. When the drawing is finished, tack the scroll to broomsticks or long cardboard tubes. The story is told or read while the scroll is held by two girls and slowly unrolled.

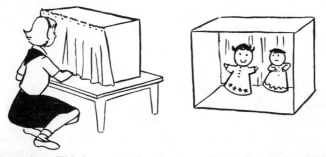

Puppetry: This is a way of acting out a story through small doll-like figures. The "puppeteer" speaks the lines, and moves the puppets from behind the scenes.

Puppets to Make

Fingerettes: This is a puppet for which one of your fingers moves the head, and two others move the arms.

Use a hollow rubber or plastic ball, or a small box, to make the head. (Potatoes, beets, socks, or sponges may also be used.) Cut a hole large enough to insert the top of your index finger. Cut features for the face out of cloth, paper, cardboard, bits of yarn, cotton, cork, sponge, or other material. Glue these to the ball. Hair and eyelashes may be made by cutting paper into strips. Curl the ends by pulling the strips between a pencil and your thumb; glue "hair" to top of the ball.

Do you prefer short hair? If so, cut a circle out of paper. Now cut strips towards the center, but not to the center. Curl the ends and glue the "hair" to the top of the head. A hat? Dressmaker scraps are dandy.

Drape a handkerchief or square piece of cloth over the top of your index finger, then insert the finger into the head of the puppet. Mark and cut two slits in the cloth for the thumb and middle finger to come through. These become the puppet's arms. Now make your puppet a lively one!

Finger Puppets: These have movable legs rather than movable arms and head. Cut out a cardboard doll figure. Instead of making legs, draw and cut two cardboard circles at the bottom of the body and about one half inch away from the edge. Insert your index and third fingers through the holes to make this puppet walk, hop, skip, and dance.

Cut Paper Puppets: These are cardboard puppets with movable joints. Cut out flat paper objects such as dolls, birds, and animals. Separate the parts such as legs, arms, wings, etc. Rejoin with a knotted cord. Decorate, and suspend on a stick. Jiggle for animated fun.

Bib Puppets: This puppet requires two people to make it work. First, tack a child's dress or suit to a curtain. Now, cut a slit in the curtain just above the collar large enough to slip your head through. Cut slits just under the sleeves (for arms) and just above the hem of the dress (for legs). Each slit should be just large enough for an arm to come through. Add strings to the collar of the dress to tie around the neck of the head poking through. For legs, cut two 10″ or 12″ pieces of broomstick and pad them with cotton. Or use cardboard tubes. Slip baby socks and shoes on the sticks and fasten securely with glue or tacks. This is how it works. One girl is the head and operates the legs. The girl who stands behind her uses her own arms as arms. In order to allow enough space for more than one puppet, fasten the costumes to the curtain about two feet apart. Be sure the curtain is hung securely, too. The action will probably get quite lively.

Bib Puppets

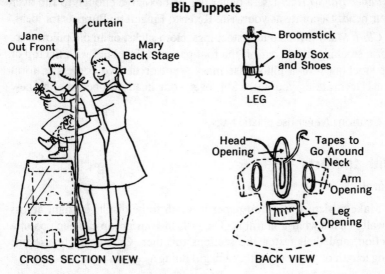

CROSS SECTION VIEW   BACK VIEW

The Puppet Stage: This may be made in any one of the following ways.

1. Stretch a cloth across a doorway. The puppets perform above this.
2. A three-sided piece of cardboard (to make it stand up) set on a table. This is portable.
3. A large picture frame with a curtain behind it.
4. A square box or carton—for very little puppets. Remove the top and bottom, and set carton on its side.

Backdrops can be large sheets of wrapping paper, cardboard, or window shades, on which a scene has been painted. A backdrop that moves is described in Scroll Show.

For between scenes or acts, paint large numbers and titles on cards and hold them up.

Props: Cardboard boxes, and cardboard with supports in the back can make a variety of furniture and other props for the set. Spice with imagination.

Light: Light the stage by using either one gooseneck lamp in front and below the stage, or two gooseneck lamps at either side of the stage.

Masks

Paper Bag Masks: Use a paper bag or box large enough to slip over your head. Decorate as you wish. Refer to Fingerette Puppets for ideas.

Cloth Mask: Make out of stockings, cloth sacks, or an old pillowcase. For a stocking mask, cut off the foot part and tie a knot with the top of the stocking. For a pillowcase mask, knot or tie two corners to form ears. Decorate as you wish. Slip over your head and become the new you.

Caution: *Never* use plastic bags.

With the Arts

Mural

Make a picture story on paper or cloth to be displayed right across a wall. That's what a mural is. The girls in your group can each paint a section, and then fasten the sections together. Or you might use one long length of paper or cloth, each girl doing a certain part.

Use interesting combinations of materials. Try paints, crayons, chalk, or pastels, with cord, yarn, cardboard, paper, wood, grasses, sticks, seeds, or plastic.

Apply the paint with brushes, sponges, rags, and plastic screw-top squeeze containers. Fasten the textured materials with glue, paste, rubber cement, clear nail polish, or needle and thread.

Painting

Colors are exciting to explore. What can you make them say? Dip a brush slightly in clean water, then in a color and start painting on paper. Clean the brush before dipping it into fresh color to keep the colors clean and clear. Discover new colors by mixing combinations right on the paper. Try these ways to paint:

- Paint areas with clean water and drop blobs of color on the area.
- Paint with a fairly dry brush; then paint another color over the first color after it has dried. Add a third color. Then, with a bobby pin, scratch designs down through the layers of paint.
- Make a light-to-dark painting.
- Make a painting of how sounds seem to you; of how music makes you feel; of the colors that make you want to dance.

- Paint colors that make you feel *happy* and ones that make you *sad*. What color would you paint if you were *excited?*
- Paint with dots and lines.

Sand Painting

This was an ancient Indian art. Look for fine examples in museums. Try making a sand painting of your own. First, mix clean white sand (or salt) with powdered tempera paint. Keep colors in separate cans. Next, lightly sketch a design in pencil on a large sheet of brown paper. Work on a flat surface (outdoors if possible). Brush thin glue over part of the design, and dribble colored sand on this glued area before it dries. Continue until your design is complete. Afterwards, spray with clear lacquer to preserve your picture.

Mosaic

This is a design made by cementing or gluing small bits of colored glass or stone onto a background. This is how you do it.

First, draw a simple design on a heavy or a lightweight board. Decide what materials you will use. Remember that heavier materials, such as stones, tile, formica, etc., must be placed on a heavier background. Mosaic materials might be: pebbles, seeds, eggshell bits, breakfast cereals, beans, peas, buttons, felt, or leather.

Now glue the little pieces to your design, keeping the outlines sharp, until the area is covered. For added firmness, and a neater look, you can use grout. Fill the crevices between the pieces with this cement-like mixture. With a damp cloth, wash off any grout from the surface design.

Clay

Whether you buy it or dig it out of the river bank, clay is fun to work with.

Squash a large handful of clay with your fingers and play with it to get the feel of it. Begin modeling by forming and smoothing the piece of clay until you make a shape you like. It might be an animal, a dish, a person, or just an imaginative shape. Dip your fingers in water to smooth out rough places in the clay. Stick shapes together by moistening a little, and roughing the edges that will touch.

A Pinch Bowl: Form a ball of clay by rolling between cupped palms. Shape bowl by pressing down the center of the clay with the thumbs. Turn clay with fingertips as you pull up the sides with the thumbs.

A Coil Bowl: Pat clay into a flat round disc to form the bottom of a bowl. Build up sides by adding layers of coils, using water and a gentle smoothing pressure to stick the coils together. With moistened fingers smooth out coils.

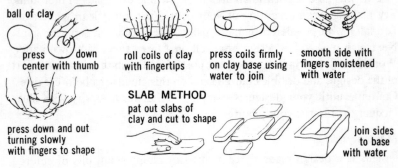

PINCH METHOD

ball of clay

press down center with thumb

roll coils of clay with fingertips

COIL METHOD

press coils firmly on clay base using water to join

smooth side with fingers moistened with water

press down and out turning slowly with fingers to shape

SLAB METHOD

pat out slabs of clay and cut to shape

join sides to base with water

A Slab Box: Pat or roll out evenly, slabs of clay to form the 4 sides and bottom of box. Put pieces together by roughing the edges. Use water as a binder. Press and smooth as you work.

Dry clay slowly, away from sun. For more exciting adventures in clay, explore glazes and clay decorating and kiln firing.

Combining Art Forms with Other Interests

Egg Show

Plan a show inside an "egg." They're fun to make and fun to see! Will it tell the Camp Fire story, your symbol story, a scene from a story the group has read, or something else? Here is how you do it.

The "egg shell": Blow up a large balloon, either oval or round. Grease the surface with vaseline. Tear paper toweling and newspaper into large strips. Keep in separate piles. Use a layer of each kind, toweling or newspaper, in turn. Cover balloon with these strips, which you have dipped into a flour-and-water paste or wall paper paste. Do this until you have made four layers; overlap the strips as you work. Be sure to keep one end free of paper, in an uneven jagged space (big enough for a hand to fit in). This will be where you will insert your "show," and peep through to view it. Dry your paper shell at room temperature, then pop the balloon and carefully remove it.

Decorating the shell: Color the inside with paint and brush, or swish a little liquid paint around inside. Decorate the outside with a symbol design or with one that carries out the theme of your "egg" show.

Placing the "show": Using tiny bits of nature materials or small cut-outs, gently insert your "scene," gluing each piece into place.

Felt Story Board

Use a board to exhibit paintings or photographs, for announcements, or to entertain a younger group. Tell a story on it, or use it as a background for a puppet show. Just slap the scenery on and off! *This is how you make it.* Cover a piece of heavy cardboard or large wood panel with a dark colored felt—or heavy flannel. The felt must be larger than the board by 3 to 4 inches all around so that you can tack it securely on the other side. Now make storybook characters, scenery, letters, or symbols to illustrate whatever you plan. These may be made from paper to which a piece of felt or sandpaper are attached on the back side so that it will stick to the felt surface. Or they can be cut from felt. It will stick by itself.

The Sky at Night

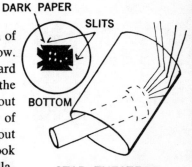

DARK PAPER

SLITS

BOTTOM

STAR THEATER

Would you like to make a constellation of stars right on your own ceiling? Here's how.

Remove the lid from a round cardboard cereal box, and decorate the outside of the box. Now cut a rectangular opening about 2″ x 1½″ in the bottom. In each corner of this rectangle, cut a small slit. Next, cut out of dark paper several 1¾″ x 3″ pieces. Look at a constellation chart, and select a constellation. Punch a hole with a nail in the dark paper for each star in this group. Then slip the paper under the slits in the rectangular opening in the bottom of the box. Hold a flashlight at an angle inside the box. Direct it at the ceiling in a darkened room. When several girls flash their constellations at the same time, you have a miniature planetarium. Can you recognize the various constellations? Have you ever been to a real planetarium? Or had a star-gazing meeting?

Umbrella Planetarium

Another way to make a planetarium is with an umbrella. This is how you do it.

Remove the fabric from an old umbrella frame, and save one gore of the fabric for a pattern. Cut as many gores out of brown wrapping paper as your umbrella requires. Lay the gores out so that you have a flat circle.

Look in a star book to find the constellations that can be seen in the heavens the month you are doing this project. Draw correctly a few of the constellations on the paper. Then punch out each star, pasting gummed reinforcements around each hole. Next, tape the gores together and place this paper cover over the umbrella frame. Girls can stand under it and see the "stars in the sky."

Look in the "Books to Help You" section at the end of this book for suggestions about many other ways to enjoy "the lively arts."

HOLD ON TO HEALTH

This is a part of the Law of the Camp Fire Girls. This is also very important to try to do, whether you are a Camp Fire Girl or not. It means: keep your body, your mind, and your ideals healthy and strong.

Prescription For Health

The proper amounts of the following will help you to do this.

> Sleep and rest
> Fresh, clean clothing—and a clean body
> Basic Four meals—three times a day!
> Clean thoughts—and a happy heart
> Work and play—the Camp Fire way
> Fresh air and sunshine
> Fitness exercises—at least five minutes every day.

Special Suggestions For Diet and Fitness

A Rosy Cheeks Diary

Make a Rosy Cheeks Diary and keep it for a month or so. Perhaps your group would like to do this together.

This is how you make it. Rule your diary like the following, but make it big enough for a whole week. Write down what you eat for each meal. Match what you eat to Basic Food Groups #1, 2, 3, or 4. See the chart in Chapter 12. In red crayon mark the Food Group number beside each food, and put a ring around it, as in the sample below. In the Exercise column mark a (5) for each five minutes of exercises you do that day. In the last column, put the number of hours you slept.

Your Rosy Cheeks Diary Might Look Like This:

Day	Breakfast	Lunch	Dinner	Snacks	Exercise	Hours of Sleep
Monday	(3) Juice (2) Egg (4) Cereal (1) & Milk (4) Toast (1) & Butter (1) Milk	(2) Peanut Butter (4) Sandwich (1) Milk (3) Carrot (3) Apple	(1) Milk (4) Bread (3) Tomato (2) Hamburger (3) Asparagus (3) Potato (1) Pudding	(1) Milk and (4) Cookies	(5)	9½

Surprise! If your Rosy Cheeks Diary shows #1, 2, 3, 4 each day for a week, you've earned honor 308 in Home Craft.

Fitness Exercises

Why exercise? It makes you stronger. It helps to work off extra pounds if you have them, makes those muscles strong and flexible, and peps you up. It also improves your skill in games and dancing, helps you sit tall, stand at ease, and walk smoothly. It gives you a graceful figure.

Games and outdoor fun help too. You will want to hold on to health both ways. Try to do the following exercises at least five minutes a day.

1. *Penny and Mouse:*

Mouse Stand with feet parallel. Roll out to the outside of the feet and curl the toes under. Heels and toes should touch so that a mouse sitting in the hollow could not escape. Return to flat foot position.

Penny Now with feet flat raise only the toes as if to expose a penny. Return to original position. Alternate Mouse and Penny. Start with 8 sets and work up to 24.

2. *Waist Twist:*

Stand with feet apart, arms held away from body. Twist body as far as possible to left and then right. Follow back hand with head and eyes. Start with eight and alternating with #3 work up to 4 sets of each.

3. *Bent Waist Twist*

Feet still apart, bend forward at the hips. Bend the elbows and do a waist twist from the bent position. Double the time that you use in #2. Start with 16 twists (= one set) and alternating with #2 work up to doing 4 sets of each.

4. *Single-Knee Bend:*

Legs wide apart, feet turned out. Bend right knee and then return to stand position; tighten seat and abdomen. Then bend left. Do 8 each side, always stopping at start position.

5. *Knee Bend Shift:*

Start with legs *very wide apart,* feet turned out. Bend right knee about half way to a full knee bent position without coming up to starting position; cross over to other leg as though there were a roof overhead. Repeat 8 times. Gradually work down to full knee bend shift.

6. *Snap and Stretch:*

Feet apart, elbows bent at shoulder level (do not let them droop). *Snap* elbows back then on next count open arms and stretch them open and back. Alternate in steady rhythm. Start with 8, work up to 16.

7. *Side Bounce:*

Feet apart, place hand on right thigh. Left hand straight up. Drop upper body over right thigh and bounce 4 times. Then 4 left.

Alternate with exercise #8 for 3 sets of each.

8. *Hamstring Stretch (Up):*

Start with legs apart, knees straight and hands behind back. Lean forward from hips, keeping back straight and head up. Bounce downward in gentle bounces 8 center, 8 right, 8 left, and 8 center.

9. *Hamstring Stretch (Down):*

Alternate with #8. Keeping legs as in #8, allow upper body to fall downward toward the floor; *relax* neck, shoulders and arms. Bounce downward but do not force; let gravity do the work. 8 center, 8 right, 8 left, 8 center.

10. *Toe Rise:*

Feet together, head and chest up, shoulders back, abdomen, seat, knees and legs held tight. Rise slowly to the toes. Count slowly 1-2-3-4. Descend at same rate. On the second rise count to 5, then 6, then 7, then 8. Come back the same way to one count for a full rise, and then do 8 lifts with one count up and one down.

"Keep Fit" — For What?

Fit to live
To enjoy life
To love and to be loved

To run fast enough to keep up with the others
To be strong enough to go out in any weather
To climb a tree, balance on a fence and ride a bike
To stand on your head—turn a cartwheel or a flip-flop

To ski, dance, swim, play tennis and climb a high mountain
To ride a horse, make a team—for the joy of belonging!

To love
To work
To succeed
To enjoy each day—all day
Fit to live.

BONNIE PRUDDEN

GAMES

Springtime
Hopscotch on the sidewalk
Marbles in the mud,
Happy children everywhere,
Lilacs are in bud.
Bare knees seek the sunshine,
Caps are tossed away,
Happy spirits fly like kites,
To greet each warm spring day.

LAUREL DOBBS
Minneapolis, Minnesota

Before-the-meeting games, quiet games, mixers, active games, make-up-your-own games, musical games, Indian games—take your choice!

Play games at each meeting. At least one game should be active. Try an old favorite, or learn a new one. A Games chairman for each meeting can plan this.

Pointers on Leading and Teaching Games:

1. Start with a game or dance everyone knows.
2. Know the game well yourself. Read directions carefully. Be sure of the rules. Think how to explain them clearly.

3. Wait! When you have attention, then announce the game or give directions. Raise your hand for quiet; others will follow.
4. Speak slowly. Keep voice low but speak to be heard.
5. Give directions in short sentences. Demonstrate when necessary.
6. Use chimes or bell for signals. (Use whistle only when group is large or you are in large outdoor area.)
7. Get into the game quickly, as soon as everyone understands.
8. Play the game yourself. Be enthusiastic. Enjoy playing. Others will follow your lead. Change the game when everyone is having a good time.

Games

Test Your Senses   Lay out different kinds of leaves and plants. Keep them covered until ready to play. Blindfold 1 girl. See how many leaves she can identify by *feeling*. After she has guessed, she helps to blindfold the others.

Play this same with vegetables. Identify their shapes. Or play it with plants, vegetables or leaves but identify them by smell. You'll find you have earned Outdoors Craft honor 131!

Seven Touches   Lay out on a table 2 articles from each of the Seven Crafts. Business Craft might be a penny, eraser, envelope; Sports and Games, a ball, bathing cap; Creative Arts, paint brush, spool of thread. Look through the honors. Think up original ideas. Keep articles covered until ready to play. Blindfold 1 girl. Lead her to table. Give her certain number of minutes to identify by feeling. Or let the group look at the table for 2 minutes; then each girl writes down as many as she can remember.

Symbol Shout   Two relay lines, facing each other. Guardian has a set of large symbol cards. She flashes 1 card and holds it where all can see. The first girl who shouts out the correct name of the symbol gains a point for her team.

Which Symbol?   Divide the group into 2 teams. Line up each team side by side facing each other, about 2 yards apart. Make a goal line about 6 yards behind each team. Give the name of a symbol to each team. The leader calls out 1 of these 2 symbols. The team whose symbol is called chases the other team, capturing as many as possible before they cross their own goal line. Those captured become part of the opposite team.

There's An Actress in Every Bag Divide group into two or more teams of actresses. Give each a paper bag containing "costume" materials (ribbons, flower, pencil, compact, bit of cloth, veil, anything). Give each team a certain number of minutes to make up a skit, story or song based on ideas from contents of bag. Each team acts out its show for the rest of the group. They can announce it or have the audience guess.

Active Games

Play an active game or two at every meeting, outdoors or in. Have a Games Chairman for each meeting. Play 1 old favorite and learn 1 new game.

Squirrel-in-Nest Divide into groups of 4. Three join hands to form a nest. The fourth girl in center is the squirrel. Choose 1 girl to be a squirrel without a nest. A leader blows a whistle or gives a signal. All squirrels must leave their nests and find another. The squirrel without a nest tries to find a home in the scramble. The one left out is the squirrel without a nest.

Left-handed Relay Two relay teams face each other. After each person puts left hand out, her left wrist is grasped by the right hand of person on her left. A ball (or other object) is passed by each left hand —all the way down to the end and back to the beginning. No one may move out of line. Hands may not be unclasped. If object is dropped, everyone stoops to help girl who dropped it.

Indian Relay Game Two teams face each other. One side has a covered can with pebbles in it, and a tight-fitting cover. (The cover is fastened on with Scotch tape or adhesive.) As someone plays music, the can is tossed back and forth between the two lines. When the music stops (or a whistle if no music) the side holding the can, or last touching it, loses 5 points.

Rolling Target Two teams are formed. Players of 1 team, each holding a bean bag, stand 5 feet apart. A leader rolls a hoop, 1 or 2 feet in diameter, the entire length of the line—at about 8 feet from the players. Those who throw the bean bag through the rolling hoop score a point for their team.

Going to Jerusalem Backwards Girls walk backwards around the row of chairs. They sit when the music *starts* to play.

Make Up Your Own Games!

These are games which groups have made up, usually from old favorites. Just for fun, try making up some new games.

One-handed Ball   This game, created by girls, is a variety of Dodge Ball. Make up your own way to play it. One group played using 1 hand only, the other held behind the back. Another group played by kicking the ball, never touching it with the hands at all.

Good Morning   The group forms a circle with It walking around the outside. It taps someone on the back. That girl walks in opposite direction. When the two meet they bow (or shake hands) and say "Good Morning." They continue walking, each trying to get to the empty space first. Substitute other things for "Good Morning" and bowing.

Musical Games

Musical Symbols   This is another "new" old game. One group made it up, like musical chairs. Fasten large paper symbols around the room on the wall. Instead of finding a chair when the music stops, each player must touch a symbol.

Guess My Song   Each girl chooses a song everyone will know. Instead of singing it, tap the rhythm of a line or two—with your feet or with a pencil, or clap your hands. The others try to guess your song.

Singing Games and Dances

You'll enjoy singing games and dances with a group of any size, or any age. The directions are usually right in the words of the songs, and they will teach you some of the basic square dance steps. Learn these and you'll be ready for American square dancing, and that's wonderful fun and exercise.

Honey, You Can't Love One

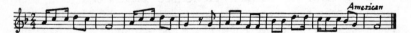

1. Honey, you can't love one, Honey, you can't love one
   You can't love one and still have fun, Honey, you can't love one.
2. —and still be true; 3. —and still have me; 4; —and love any more; 5. —and come out alive; 6. and not be in a fix (make up your own from here).

Step: A leisurely strolling walk.

Formation and Action: 1st verse—Four girls join right hands to form a star in center of the floor, and stroll around clockwise while all others sing in large circle facing in.

2nd verse—Girls face about, join left hands and march counter-clockwise, and each beckons to a boy who joins her, links arms and wheels with her.

3rd verse—All drop hands, face about, girls join right hands, others link arms, wheel slowly and players on outside of spokes of wheel beckon to player of opposite sex to join them.

This facing, wheeling and beckoning are continued until all are participating or until the last verse is sung. Players near center must move more slowly as spokes grow in size.

(From *Musical Mixers*, National Recreation Association)

Brown-Eyed Mary

American

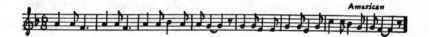

1. If perchance we should meet on the wild, wild prairie,
   In my arms I will embrace my darling brown eyed Mary.
2. Turn your partner half way 'round, turn your opposite lady,
   Turn your partner all around, and prom'nade right hand lady.

Formation: Double circle, boy on the inside, girl on his right, hands crossed as in skating position.

Action: 1st verse — Partners promenade in a circle, two steps to each measure.

2nd verse — Partners join right hands and turn half around, so that boy is facing back, with right hand toward center, girl in opposite direction .... 2 measures

Each boy joins left hands with the girl who was in the couple behind him and turns her completely around.............................. 2 measures

Joining right hands with original partner, turns her entirely around
2 measures

Take girl behind in promenade position for new partner and repeat from beginning .... 2 measures

Ach Ja!

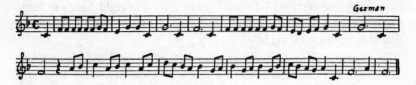

My father and my mother take us to the fair
Ach Ja, Ach Ja
We haven't any money, and it's little that we care
Ach Ja, Ach Ja
Tra la la, tra la la, tra la la la la la la
Tra la la, tra la la, tra la la la la la la
Ach Ja! Ach Ja!

Formation: Partners in double circle, counter-clockwise, boys on inside of circle, inside hands joined.

Action: Stroll 8 steps.. 2 measures

Drop hands, partners face each other and bow   1 measure

Partners turn to their left and bow at others
in circle .... 1 measure

Repeat all ....next four measures

Girl steps in front of partner, back to him; they
clasp hands shoulder high, take 4 slides to
center circle, 4 slides out................................ 4 measures

Partners drop hands, girl moves to position
beside partner, face and bow.......................... 1 measure

Boys move forward around circle to new part-
ner, and dance continues................................ 1 measure

Rig-a-jig-jig

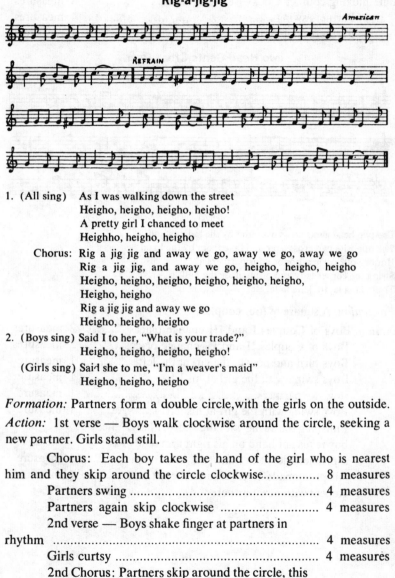

American

1. **(All sing)** As I was walking down the street
     Heigho, heigho, heigho, heigho!
     A pretty girl I chanced to meet
     Heighho, heigho, heigho

   Chorus: Rig a jig jig and away we go, away we go, away we go
     Rig a jig jig, and away we go, heigho, heigho, heigho
     Heigho, heigho, heigho, heigho, heigho, heigho,
     Heigho, heigho
     Rig a jig jig and away we go
     Heigho, heigho, heigho

2. **(Boys sing)** Said I to her, "What is your trade?"
     Heigho, heigho, heigho, heigho!

   (Girls sing) Said she to me, "I'm a weaver's maid"
     Heigho, heigho, heigho

Formation: Partners form a double circle, with the girls on the outside.

Action: 1st verse — Boys walk clockwise around the circle, seeking a new partner. Girls stand still.

    Chorus: Each boy takes the hand of the girl who is nearest him and they skip around the circle clockwise .... 8 measures

        Partners swing .... 4 measures

        Partners again skip clockwise .... 4 measures

        2nd verse — Boys shake finger at partners in

rhythm .... 4 measures

        Girls curtsy .... 4 measures

        2nd Chorus: Partners skip around the circle, this

time moving counter-clockwise .... 8 measures
       Partners swing .... 4 measures
       Partners skip counter-clockwise .... 4 measures

Two Head Gents Cross Over

The two head gents cross over and by the ladies stand
The opposite two cross over and take them by the hand
Honor your corner, honor your partners all
Swing the corner lady and promenade the hall
Tra la la la la, tra la la la la, etc.

Formation: A square of four couples.

Action: Boys of Couples I and III change places .... 2 measures
       Boys of Couples II and IV change places............ 2 measures
       Boys turn and bow to the girl at the left................ 1 measure
       Boys swing with the girl at his left........................ 1 measure
       Bow to partners.. 1 measure
       Boys swing with the girl at his left........................ 1 measure
       Finishing the swing with the "corner lady," the
       boy takes her hand on his right arm ready for
       a promenade.. 1 measure
       All promenade once around the set.................... 4 measures
       Repeat with new partner.

CHAPTER 18

FRIENDSHIP ACROSS THE SEAS

The Meaning of Friendship in Camp Fire

". . . For I will tend as my fathers have tended
And my fathers' fathers since time began
The fire that is called the love of man for man
The love of man for God."

These words from the Fire Maker's Desire tell what friendship means to a Camp Fire Girl. "Love of man for man" means learning to love, understand and appreciate *all* people—in your own home, in your Camp Fire group, in your neighborhood, in other places. "Love of man for God" means that you respect the right of everyone to worship God according to his own Faith.

Friendship is a far-reaching word. The world is full of people we would like—if only we knew them. So let's get acquainted!

People from far-away nations seem like "next-door neighbors" today, because you see them, their homes, and their countries on television. You hear children's voices and songs and chatter. You see their costumes, their dances and celebrations. Jet air travel brings friends to us from across the seas—quickly and often. It takes friends from this country to visit other nations.

Sometimes families from other countries come here to live. Then you have the wonderful fun of getting to know them, in school and in your neighborhood. Are you lucky enough to have one of these girls as a member of your Camp Fire group? What can you do to make her feel she belongs, right away? Can you tell her that the Indians are really the original Americans? That everyone else in America came from across the seas like her, at some time—perhaps long ago? Help her to learn your songs and games and all about Camp Fire. Welcome her.

Paths to Friendship

Make a friendship ring around the world. There are ways to get to know and learn about friends in other countries, even from afar. You and your group might like to try several of the following suggestions.

· *Plan a magic carpet trip to another section of the world.* "Visit" two or three countries. What kind of clothing would you wear? What special things would you like to see while you were there? What kinds of foods would you be served? What would you do? How would you go, and how long would it take if you really went to those countries?

· *Visit a travel agency, a steamship or airlines office,* and ask for travel folders and posters from other countries. Have a special travel party: each girl, or groups of three or four, can explain why they are traveling to a particular country.

· *Visit a museum.* See what its arts and crafts can tell you about other countries.

· *Plan to serve foods from other countries,* at one or two of your group meetings.

· *Have an international songfest.* Each girl can learn one folk song of another country. (Choose different ones.) *Music Makers* (Cat. No. D-79) is a good resource. Teach your group the song you learned, and you'll have an around-the-world "sing."

· *See a foreign language movie with your group;* talk about it at your meeting.

· *On television, see and hear about children and people in other countries.* Tell your group about what you've seen.

· *"Adopt" a country.* Set up an exhibit of it, with drawings and pictures from magazines, or with photographs. Show how families live in that country. Then write a short play about them.

- *Read about children in other lands.* Find out about their cultural backgrounds by reading legends and other stories written by local authors. Ask your librarian about finding these books. She can also suggest more that tell about children's home life in other countries. Use them for storytelling and dramatizations.

- *Find a pen friend.* Pen friends often become lifetime friends! Camp Fire Girls has a *Pen Friends* leaflet, which you may have. It gives some hints on how to be a good pen friend, and where you may write to get a name.

  Look in the chapter, "National Projects and Special Honors," to see how you can earn the national Pen Friends project honor.

- *Give service to people overseas* as well as to those who live near you. This is usually done through approved agencies. Your guardian can find out about these agencies for you. They may have offices in your own town.

  If you are planning to Give Service to friends near and/or far, you will be on your way toward *Project Share.* Check its requirements in the *"Project Share Honors"* chapter.

- *Observe October 24th as United Nations Day* in ways such as these:

  1. Find out about the United Nations, and the work of UNICEF. Do you know what the initials UNICEF mean?

  2. Although groups may *not collect* money for other organizations, you may contribute pennies from your group treasury. (One penny provides five glasses of milk to a child overseas. Five pennies mean a glass of milk a day for nearly a month.)

  3. Make posters about UNICEF's work, to be used in stores, banks, airports, railroad and bus stations.

  4. Become acquainted with the UNICEF *Hi Neighbor!* books. They tell you about songs, dances, games, stories, and crafts from other countries that you can try too. These books can be ordered from U.S. Committee for UNICEF, 331 East 38th Street, New York, N. Y. 10016.

- *Go globe-trotting with postage stamps.* At a meeting, make plans to show stamps the girls have collected. Or invite someone who has a stamp collection to show it to you. Have a stamp swap. Tell something about each stamp, its country, and what it represents.

• *Find someone who has lived or traveled in another country.* Invite this person to be your guest at a group meeting, and to tell about the country and its children. Do they go to camp? Do they roller skate? What are their favorite games? Are their homes near the sea or the mountains? What kind of flowers grow there? Birds? See how many things you can think of that we use, wear or eat, that comes from that country. Try to learn a folk song and dance. Can you sing the song in the language of that country? Can you give your guest a greeting in that language?

CHAPTER 19

NATIONAL PROJECTS AND SPECIAL HONORS

National Projects

National projects mean more fun for you and your group, and more ways for you to "Give Service", the slogan of Camp Fire Girls. Blue Birds, Camp Fire Girls, Junior Hi Camp Fire Girls, and Horizon Club members take part in these interesting projects. It's fun to think that groups all sizes, all ages, and all places across the country are enjoying them too.

Here are the projects, and with each is a drawing of the honor girls can receive for completing it. These will look attractive on your ceremonial jacket or gown.

NOTE: Although girls participate in these national projects more than once, it seems most practical *not* to apply for any one honor more than once. Blue Birds, you remember, do not earn honors.

Pen Friends

• Find a pen friend, either in this country or abroad. Agencies which provide names and addresses of pen friends, and offer some good letter-writing tips besides, can be found in the Camp Fire Girls leaflet, *Pen Friends*. It's just for you! Request this from the council office. Otherwise your guardian may order it from Supply Division.

• Exchange at least two letters with your pen friend; share them at group meetings.

NOTE: Each girl gets her own pen friend, and pays any small fee which may be charged by the letter-writing agency for this service.

Pen Friends Honor

An *ocean blue* one-inch wooden disk, with *white* symbols for "paths crossing." (Cat. No. B-128)

Keep America Beautiful

• With your group, take part in a local project which promotes making your community more beautiful. This may be an anti-litter campaign, special location cleanup, planting of seedlings, making neighboring blocks in the community more beautiful, taking part in a public exhibit or display. This may be a single group, intergroup, or communitywide project.

NOTE: For these activities, your guardian will always obtain clearance from the council or Camp Fire Girls association.

Keep America Beautiful Honor

A *bright green* one-inch wooden disk, with *white* symbols for "earth" and "sky." (Cat. No. B-129)

Project Share

- With your group, explore situations in your home town (or in the world) which need immediate attention. Think of ways in which you and your group might be able to help solve part of the problem.
- Share your time wisely by having a project which will allow you to work with people from varied backgrounds and geographical areas.
- Plan activities which serve a definite purpose: restoring toys for distribution, tutoring children in reading and writing, teaching new games to inner-city youth, reading aloud to the blind, etc.
- Make sure that anything you contribute is in excellent condition and is packed to meet all mailing requirements, if it is being sent.

Recommended organizations through which Camp Fire Girls give service are:
— American Friends Service Committee, Children's Program, 160 North 15th St., Philadelphia, Pa. 19102
— Save the Children Federation (address: Director of Group Relations), Boston Post Road, Norwalk, Conn.
— Church World Service, National Council of Churches of Christ, 475 Riverside Drive, New York, N. Y.
— World Federation of YMHA and Jewish Community Centers, 145 East 32nd Street, New York 16, N. Y.
— Catholic Relief Services, N.C.W.C., 350 Fifth Avenue, New York, N. Y.
— Foster Parents Plan, 352 Park Avenue South, New York 10, N. Y.

Project Share Honor

A *red* one-inch wooden disk, with *white* symbols for "heart" and "person." (Cat. No. B-126)

Edith M. Kempthorne Project

- With your group, plan a celebration to honor Edith M. Kempthorne, known as "Alaska" to the Camp Fire Girls family. Base this on the leaflet, "Honor to a Great Lady," available from the council office, or if none, from Division of Program Services at national headquarters. Your guardian may send for this. The celebration might be a tea, a play, skit, or a special ceremonial.

• Each girl contributes the number of pennies equaling her age, or the total may be taken from the group treasury. This amount is sent by your guardian to the Edith M. Kempthorne Fund, Camp Fire Girls, Inc. This Fund, honoring "Alaska," helps to expand the Camp Fire Girls program and offers it to more girls all over the country.

Edith M. Kempthorne Honor

A *purple* one-inch wooden disk, with a *white* symbol *for* "woman-person." (Cat. No. B-127)

Needlework Guild

• With your group, participate in a sewing project in which new garments are made and given to those in the community in need of such help and comfort. The number of articles to be completed is left to the good judgment of the group and the leader.

• Agencies in your community can assist your group in arranging to make the contributions.

• Your group makes a monetary contribution, not less than $1.00, to The Needlework Guild of America, Inc., 124 South 12th Street, Philadelphia, Pa., 19107. The Guild presents service pins or membership cards to girls for participation in the project.

Your guardian can request the leaflet "The Camp Fire Girls and The Needlework Guild of America, Inc.," either from the council office or, if none, from Supply Division. The leaflet gives detailed information on how to carry out this project.

Needlework Guild Honor

An *aqua* one-inch wooden disk, with *white* symbols for "heart" and "hand." (Cat. No. B-130)

National Honors

Membership Honors

There are honors for girls who have had three, five, seven, and ten years as registered members in Camp Fire Girls.

Three-year Membership Honor

A *red* one-inch plastic disk, with *black* symbols for "person" in "tent."

Five-year Membership Honor

Two *red* ½-inch plastic squares, with *black* symbol for "feather."

Seven-year Membership Honor

A *silver finish* one-inch triangular (flame shape) charm, with six *red* enamel "flame" symbols.

Ten-year Membership Honor

A *silver finish* one-inch leaf-shaped charm, with 9 raised leaves.

If you believe you are eligible for one of these honors, talk to your guardian. She will know how to apply for it.

National Lifesaving Award

This award is made to a Camp Fire Girl when evidence presented to the National Awards Committee shows that she used presence of mind and good judgement in her actions, in cases such as rescuing someone from drowning or from a fire, etc.

A written account of the rescue, signed statements from two eye-witnesses (adults) and if possible, a statement from the attending nurse or doctor, must accompany the letter to the National Awards Committee applying for this award. These materials should be sent within a short time following the incident described.

Application for the award is made by the executive director or president of a council, or through the chairman of a Camp Fire Girls association. Guardians of lone groups send the information to: National Awards Committee, Camp Fire Girls, Inc., 65 Worth Street, New York, N. Y. 10013.

A *navy blue* two-inch felt square, with *red* symbol for "person."

NOTE: Requests for *all* honors in the Camp Fire Girls program are made by your guardian. Ask her, if you think you have earned the right to obtain any of the honors.

CHAPTER 20

SAFETY FIRST—AND LAST

As you grow, you learn about safety and how to take responsibility for it. Camp Fire Girls help younger children and older people by taking these safety precautions.

The most important thing is to *think*. Use your head! Understand why safety rules are necessary. Observe them.

Safety on City Streets

- Cross streets only at intersections, not diagonally.
- Look both ways before crossing.
- Watch for cars at driveways and alleys. Watch for turning cars.
- Do not walk between parked cars.
- Do not play in the street. Do not dash into the street after anything.
- Be even more careful on rainy days and after dark.
- Never walk alone at night. Have an adult with you. Wear something white or carry a flashlight.
- Look where you are walking. Don't hide under an umbrella or behind a big package.
- Watch and obey police officers, safety patrols, traffic signals.

Safety on Country Roads

You'll find suggestions for safety in hiking, fire building, and outdoor cooking in Chapter 13. Think about and follow these safety pointers when walking or hiking along a country road:

- Walk on *left* side of road, facing traffic. This is so you can see what is coming. You can see the cars better than the drivers can see you!
- Watch out for passing cars, and for cars coming from behind you.
- Never walk after dark without an adult.
- Wear something white or carry a flashlight if you must be on the road after dark. Ask the adult with you to do the same.
- Remember a car cannot stop instantly, even if the driver sees you. You *can* stop. So help the motorist and avoid accidents by keeping out of the traffic lane.

- Get off the highway when a car approaches or when you stop to rest.
- Keep your group close together. Take up as little of the road as possible.
- Look both ways before crossing railroad tracks; cross only at regular crossings. Never walk on rails or ties.

Safety for Bicycle Riders

Your Bicycle

- Keep bicycle in good order at all times. Check this list of reminders:
- Wheels—run smoothly and true; spokes in good condition
- Seat—proper height and fastened tight
- Handle bars—adjusted properly; grips tight
- Tires—properly inflated; no tape or puncture
- Chain—proper tension and guarded
- Pedals—oiled; in good condition
- Brakes—test often; important!
- Signals and lights—securely fastened and working
- Basket or rack (if used)—firmly attached
- License holder visible
- Reflector on rear

You the Rider

No bike is safer than the girl who rides it! Follow these simple safety rules:

- Obey traffic signs—lights, stop signs, one-way streets.
- Keep to the right in single line. Don't stunt!
- Have white headlight, rear reflector, and horn or bell.
- Give pedestrians right of way. Do not ride on sidewalks.
- Look out for cars pulling out from curb into traffic.
- Never ride two on a bicycle. Never hitch on a vehicle.
- Be sure your brakes are working well.
- Walk your bike across busy intersections. Look both ways before crossing.
- Stop at street when riding out of alleys or driveways.
- Learn hand signals and use them before stopping or turning.

- Do not weave in and out on the road. Ride straight.
- Keep both hands on handle bars for steering.
- Park your bike in a safe place. Turn wheel so bike can't fall, or stand it where others won't fall over it or into it.

A Bike Safety Meeting. Ask someone to meet with your group to discuss and demonstrate safety rules, and check your bikes' safety.

Safety for Roller Skaters

Roller skating is fun any time of year. It's good exercise too. Here are some safety tips.

- Keep skates in good order.
- Skate on sidewalk, never in the street.
- Skate on sidewalks free from bumps and cracks.
- Always skate away from busy intersections.
- Be on the alert for cars coming out of driveways and alleys.
- Never skate hitched to a vehicle.
- Keep hands free to keep balance.
- Have a safe storage place for skates.

Safety During a Money-Earning Sale

A sale gives you fine practice in learning business procedures and in meeting the public. Good safety rules are important too. Councils sometimes make special rules about sales.

These safety rules apply everywhere:

- Sell only a Camp Fire Girls identified product.
- Team up with another girl; sell in pairs.
- Younger girls should sell on one side of street at a time; do not cross street while selling.
- Sell in your own neighborhood.
- Do not go into strange neighborhoods, unless an adult is with you.
- Do not sell after dark, unless accompanied by an adult.
- *Never* enter a house or apartment. Remain at the door.
- Never sell in an office building unless an adult is with you all of the time, and permission has been given in advance. The same is true for large apartment buildings.

• Do not accept any money except for a direct sale. Accept no gifts.
• Always wear Camp Fire service costume.

Safety in Winter

Wintertime is fun time. Be prepared for the weather. Know the rules for winter safety.

For Ice Skaters

• Use sharp skates. Keep blades covered when skates are not in use.
• Wait until ice is frozen at least four inches thick. Always have approval from your parent or guardian before you go onto the ice.
• Do not skate alone. Do not skate after dark, unless the rink is well lighted.
• Skate from your hips down; keep your weight headed into direction you are traveling. Bend your knees and lean forward to avoid a backward fall.

On Sleds

• Watch out for trees and other stationary objects.
• In case of unavoidable collision, it is usually best to roll off your sled.
• Do not cross the coasting path on foot.
• Sleds should not be overloaded.
• Never slide on streets that are not roped off!
• Never hitch sled behind automobiles.

For Skiers

• Use proper equipment that is in good condition.
• Use skis of proper length, strength and flexibility. (The usual length is 10 inches more than your height.)
• Learn to ski correctly.
• Use trails and slopes within your ability.
• Do not ski alone.
• Rest often. Fatigue is a large factor in accidents.
• Carry skis over your shoulder, points down.

Invite an expert skier to visit your group and demonstrate the proper equipment, how to wear it, use it, and take care of it. Make up a list of questions to ask about the above safety suggestions.

Fire Safety

Follow these Rules

1. Keep calm!
2. *Call Fire Department at once.*
   Tell *where* the fire is.
3. Never open a door which feels warm or hot. Find another way out.
4. If your clothing catches fire, NEVER RUN. Wrap yourself in blanket or rug to smother flames.
5. Know where nearest fire alarm box is, if there is one in your neighborhood.

Learn and discuss these tips with your parents and your group.

Have a Fire Prevention Meeting. Invite someone from your Fire Department to talk with your group and demonstrate what you can do in case of fire.

Other Safety Signals

On Bus Trips or in Cars

Always stay in your seat. Keep hands, arms and head inside car or bus windows. Use safety belts if available. Lock all doors.

Meeting Strangers

"No, thank you!" is the firm answer to give any strangers who might ask you to go with them on foot or in a car.

"No, thank you!" is the answer to give any stranger who offers you candy, toys or money. Tell a policeman about this immediately.

Playing with Plastic Bags

Many vegetables and fruits come in plastic bags. These can be used again for keeping things clean. Clothes come from the cleaners in plastic garment covers. Never use these for costumes! Never put them over your head, or over anyone else's head! Tell other children about this "safety signal."

At Home·

Learn that anything marked *Poison* means "Hands Off!" Don't touch it, even in play!

At Play

Never play games in old refrigerators or trunks or cars. Safety first; stop accidents *before* they happen.

More Things To Do For Safety

A First Aid Meeting

Invite an American Red Cross First Aid instructor to meet with your group. Discuss what girls your ages should do if a person faints; what to do for a cut, burn, sprain. Find out how and when to use a triangular bandage. What would you do for a nosebleed, a blister, something in your eye, for frost bite, sunburn, a splinter? Find out what goes into an adequate first aid kit for your home, for the hike, for your automobile.

A Safety Expert Hunt

Make a list of safety experts in your community who watch out for the safety of people, animals, and property. (The fire chief, police chief, someone from the nearest school, church, hospital, health department . . . who else?)

Invite some safety experts to visit your group. Make appointments for your group to visit others. Ask them about their jobs and how you can help with safety.

Emergency Calls

Learn and act out how to call an ambulance, the Fire Department, the police, the doctor, the health department. What information should you give in case of emergency?

Always remember "Safety First" — and last!

Part 4

TAKE A FORWARD LOOK

WHAT COMES NEXT IN CAMP FIRE GIRLS

Before you were in Camp Fire, you probably were a Blue Bird. If you were, you were happy making your Blue Bird Wish come true, and being a part of the big Camp Fire Girls family.

When you are twelve or in the seventh grade, you will be ready to step up to enjoy the two-year program level for Junior Hi Camp Fire Girls. Your group program will include more teen-age activities and more program with other groups.

The Junior Hi Camp Fire Girls Program

There are three basic parts to the Junior Hi Camp Fire Girls program: the fourth rank, the fifth rank, and special, more advanced honors in the Seven Crafts.

The Group Torch Bearer rank, which is the fourth rank, includes choices of activities in seven areas: Home, Arts, Science, Service, Sports and Games, Outdoors, and Party Fun. These are group choices and group activities. It is a rank which you achieve *with* others.

The *individual* Torch Bearer rank is the fifth rank. In this, there are *twenty-six* fields of interest from which you may choose! You may go on to achieve this rank in more than one field if you wish, but it is wise to work on only one at a time. You can continue working on individual Torch Bearers in Horizon Club.

The individual Torch Bearer rank offers you these fields of interest:

Aerospace
Business
Citizenship
Cooking
Dancing
Dramatics
Folk Lore
Games and Sports
Gardening
Hand Arts
Horsemanship
Indian Lore
Interior Decorating
International
    Relations

Music
Nature and
    Conservation
Needlework
Outdoor Living
Photography
Reading
Public Relations
Religious Growth
Science
Small Craft
Swimming
Your Special
    Interest

The Horizon Club Program

When you are fourteen or in the ninth grade in school, Horizon Club will be waiting. All through high school, you're growing up, and the Horizon Club program is just for you!

In Horizon Club, you'll be interested in more grown-up things. Developing a good adult personality, practicing social skills, enjoying co-ed activities, exploring career possibilities, and giving personal service to your community — these are what Horizon Club is about.

This is the time too, when you and your friends become a *club,* not a group, and you have an *adviser,* not a guardian. That is because every one agrees you are growing up, and will take the major responsibility yourselves, for your group plans and activities. Doesn't it almost make you feel grown up already, just thinking about all the fun ahead of you in Camp Fire Girls?

In addition to working in new fields on individual Torch Bearer rank, or instead, you may wish to work toward achieving the Wohelo Medallion. This is not a rank but a very special award, which takes two full years to complete. It is a symbol of personal achievement and growth, and of outstanding skilled service to others.

Giving service in grown-up ways is important to Horizon Club girls. You may do this in several ways: as an individual or with your club, as a Horizon Club Community Service Volunteer, or as an assistant Blue Bird leader or assistant Camp Fire guardian (when you are sixteen). You receive training for service, arranged by your local council.

After Horizon Club

Even in college, in business, or as young homemakers, Camp Fire Girls find their life guided by the ideals expressed in the Law of the Camp Fire Girls. Often they want to help other girls have the good times they had themselves. And what could be more wonderful than becoming a Camp Fire Girls leader? Or a camp counselor? Or someday, working in a Camp Fire Girls council?

Think of all the grownups you know who have helped you and your group: your guardian, your sponsors, your parents, the people who arrange for district or council events. You can probably think of many more. There's a place for everyone in Camp Fire Girls.

When you're an adult, you can continue membership in Camp Fire Girls by being an alumni member. The dues are $2.00 and the membership is open to all former Camp Fire Girls (beginning at 18 years of age), former leaders, assistants, sponsors, administrative volunteers, and staff, both men and women.

THE CAMP FIRE GIRLS ORGANIZATION

*(This chapter is of interest to your parents and other adults,
as well as to you)*

Are there other girls in your neighborhood who would like to be Camp Fire Girls? Or perhaps you are moving to another place and want to find a Camp Fire group to join. What to do?

Ask your mother or father or your religious leader to call the Camp Fire Girls office in your city. If Camp Fire Girls is not listed in your telephone book, ask an adult to write to Division of Field Services, Camp Fire Girls, Inc., 65 Worth Street, New York, N. Y. 10013, to request help in organizing a group.

Camp Fire Girls has three levels of organization: your group, your council or Camp Fire Girls association (in your community or area), and nationally.

Your Group

You become acquainted with Camp Fire Girls through your group. A Camp Fire group has about twelve girls, and never more than twenty.

The Group Guardian

She is a woman at least eighteen years of age, but preferably older. She is someone who loves girls and likes to work and play with them.

She might be a mother, a teacher, someone at your church or synagogue, an older sister, an aunt or a friend.

Guardians receive leadership training from the council and attend leaders and sponsors association meetings to help them become skilled guardians. In addition, many materials for further help are available to them. They find these listed in the *Handbook for Guardians of Camp Fire Girls* (Cat. No. D-71).

Sponsors

These people are a necessary part of every group. They are mothers, fathers, teachers, neighbors, or other adults who are interested in girls. They often find the guardian for the group, and watch over and help the group in many ways. They make sure the girls have a place to meet, they help with special projects and activities, and when it comes time to review your achievements for Camp Fire ranks, they help your guardian with this too. Often parent groups, service and women's clubs, churches, synagogues, and other institutions or organizations help to organize Camp Fire groups and provide sponsors for them. Every group must have at least one sponsor.

Councils *may* set up local rules about the number of additional sponsors a group should have, but no more than five.

Camp Fire Girls Council or Association

The next level of organization is the Camp Fire Girls council or Camp Fire Girls association. This is a group of men and women who are enthusiastic about Camp Fire Girls and want to help girls belong. They apply to national headquarters for an official charter. This entitles them to organize new groups and give training to guardians so that more girls can be members. They help Camp Fire Girls have camping experiences. They serve on committees and boards, and work with the community fund-raising organization. They do many other things too!

If there is no council or association in a community, Camp Fire groups may be organized independently. These are chartered groups not under council and receive help from national headquarters, and from the national Camp Fire Girls field staff members assigned to their region.

Camp Fire Girls National Organization

The third level of organization is the Camp Fire Girls national organization. This is what you have joined when you pay your national annual dues. Camp Fire Girls, Inc., which is the name of this national voluntary organization, makes the Camp Fire Girls program available, and sets policies and practices to assure that it is carried out in the way most beneficial for girls. It tells the Camp Fire Girls story across the country, in magazines and on radio and TV. It develops new materials and program helps for use in groups and in councils. It serves communities and represents them in keeping high the standards and pride of belonging to Camp Fire Girls.

The money from girls and grownups' national dues goes to the national headquarters of Camp Fire Girls to be used in all the ways mentioned above—and more. Camp Fire Girls national headquarters is located at 65 Worth Street, New York, N. Y. 10013.

Did you know that when you become a registered member your name is registered at headquarters? It has a place among the files and files of other Camp Fire Girls living all over the country. Girls and groups who visit headquarters delight in seeing *their* name and *their* group's registration among all those others.

By the way, Camp Fire Girls, their families and their friends are always welcome to visit national headquarters. To announce your arrival, a postcard or a telephone call when you're near would be appreciated. The welcome mat is always out for you!

Part 5

AND DON'T FORGET—

Books to Help You and Your Group
Your Camp Fire Record

BOOKS TO HELP YOU AND YOUR GROUP

Your group will wish to purchase some of these books. Some you'll find in your public library. As you explore new honors activities, show your *Book of the Camp Fire Girls* to your librarian. Ask her to suggest other books too that will help you.

Publications of Camp Fire Girls, Inc.

For You

Book of the Camp Fire Girls (Cat. No. D-70)
Secretary's Book (Cat. No. E-95)
Treasurer's Book (Cat. No. E-92)
Music Makers (Cat. No. D-79)
Songs for the Camp Fire Girls (Cat. No. D-90)
Our Songs (Cat. No. D-89)
Sing High, Sing Low (Cat. No. D-78)
Your Own Book of Campcraft (Cat. No. D-233)
The Name Book (Cat. No. D-73)

For Your Guardian and You to Share

The Outdoor Book (Cat. No. D-80)
Conservation (Cat. No. D-249)
Ceremonials for Camp Fire Girls (Cat. No. D-73)
Your Symbol Book (Cat. No. D-75)
Wo-He-Lo, The Story of Camp Fire Girls, 1910-1960 (Cat. No. D-277)

For Your Guardian

Handbook for Guardians of Camp Fire Girls (Cat. No. D-71)
Leads for Leaders (list of helpful books) (Cat. No. D-301)
Record Book for Groups (Cat. No. E-114) Filler. (Cat. No. E-111) Binder
The Camp Fire Girl (a magazine for adults of Camp Fire Girls; every registered guardian and assistant guardian receives a copy.)

To Purchase

All the above books, (but *not* the magazine) may be purchased from your local store which carries Camp Fire Girls supplies, or if not available there, from your council's office. Only if neither is accessible, order from Camp Fire Girls Supply Division, 450 Avenue of the Americas, New York, N. Y. 10011.

Other Books To Help You

Citizenship

Put Democracy to Work, by Ruth H. Wagner. Abelard-Schuman, New York.

Creative Arts

Art is Everywhere, by Leonard Kessler. Dodd Mead & Co., New York.

Child's Book of Sewing, by Jane Chapman. Birk & Co., Inc., 3 West 57th Street, New York. (25¢ direct from publisher)

Clay, Wood and Wire, by Harvey Weiss. William R. Scott, Inc., New York.

Collect, Print and Paint from Nature, by John Hawkinson. Albert Whitman & Co., Chicago, Ill.

Let's Play a Story, by Elizabeth Allstrom. Friendship Press, New York.

Make Your Own Musical Instruments, by Muriel Mandell, Robert E. Wood. Sterling Publishing Co., Inc., New York, N. Y.

McCall's Make-It Book, by John Peter. Golden Press, New York.

Home

Party ABCs, by Bernice Bryant. Bobbs-Merrill Company, Inc., Indianapolis and New York.

Children's Festivals from Many Lands, by Nina Millen. Friendship Press, New York.

Indians

Golden Book of Indian Crafts and Lore, by Ben Hunt. Golden Press, New York.

Book of Indian Life Crafts, by Oscar E. Norbeck, Association Press, New York.

The North American Indians, by Ernest Berke. Doubleday and Company, Inc., Garden City, New York.

Outdoors

The First Book of Gardening, by Virginia Kirkus. Franklin Watts, Inc., New York.

Golden Book of Camping and Camp Crafts, by Gordon Lynn. Golden Press, New York.

Golden Book of Nature Crafts, by John R. Saunders. Golden Press, New York.

An Introduction to Nature, by Richard Martin. Blandford Press, London.

The Junior Book of Camping and Woodcraft, by Bernard S. Mason. A. S. Barnes & Co., New Jersey.

Nature in Recreation, by Marguerite Ickis. A. S. Barnes & Co., New York.

The Wonderful World of Nature, by Mary Phillips. Viking Press, New York.

Sports and Games

Ready or Not—Here I Come, by Carl Withers, Garry Mackenzie. Grosset and Dunlap, New York.

Science

Mr. Wizard's Experiments for Young Scientists, by Don Herbert. Doubleday & Co., Inc., Garden City, New York.

101 Science Experiments, by Illa Podendorf. Children's Press, Chicago.

Research Adventures for Young Scientists, by George Barr. McGraw-Hill Book Co., New York.

Pamphlets

Information and pamphlets are available from these agencies:

Bicycle Institute of America, 122 East 42nd Street, New York.

National Safety Council, 425 North Michigan Avenue, Chicago, Ill.

National Dairy Council: Write to your local branch. If none, write to National Dairy Council, 111 North Canal St., Chicago, Ill.

RECORD OF MY HONOR ACHIEVEMENTS

To be initialed by your mother, guardian, teacher, camp counselor or other adult who knows you earned this honor.*

CRAFT and HONOR No.	What I Did to Earn an Honor	For fun draw a pictograph of the honor	Initials of Adult *	Date Beads Received
101 Bus.	Saved my allowance money.			
109 Bus.	Washed car			

RECORD OF MY HONOR ACHIEVEMENTS

To be initialed by your mother, guardian, teacher, camp counselor or other adult who knows you earned this honor.*

CRAFT and HONOR No.	What I Did to Earn an Honor	For fun draw a pictograph of the honor	Initials of Adult *	Date Beads Received

RECORD OF MY HONOR ACHIEVEMENTS

To be initialed by your mother, guardian, teacher, camp counselor or other adult who knows you earned this honor.*

CRAFT and HONOR No.	What I Did to Earn an Honor	For fun draw a pictograph of the honor	Initials of Adult *	Date Beads Received

RECORD OF MY HONOR ACHIEVEMENTS

To be initialed by your mother, guardian, teacher, camp counselor or other adult who knows you earned this honor.*

CRAFT and HONOR No.	What I Did to Earn an Honor	For fun draw a pictograph of the honor	Initials of Adult *	Date Beads Received

A RECORD OF
"MAKING MY DREAMS COME TRUE"
IN CAMP FIRE

"I DESIRE
TO SEEK THE WAY
THAT SHALL BECOME
A DELIGHT TO MY FEET...."

I became a Trail Seeker at our group ceremonial held in _____ on _____.

_____
Signature of my Camp Fire guardian.

"I WILL STRIVE TO GROW
STRONG LIKE THE PINE TREE.
TO BE PURE IN MY
    DEEPEST DESIRE;
TO BE TRUE TO THE TRUTH
    THAT IS IN ME
AND FOLLOW THE
    LAW OF CAMP FIRE."

I became a Wood Gatherer at our group ceremonial held in _____ on _____.

_____
Signature of my Camp Fire guardian.

"SO I PURPOSE TO BRING
MY STRENGTH
MY AMBITION
MY HEART'S DESIRE...."

I became a Fire Maker at a ceremonial held in _____ on _____.

_____
Signature of my Camp Fire guardian.

WHEN I'M TWELVE I'LL BE A JUNIOR HI CAMP FIRE GIRL!

INDEX

NOTES

NOTES

NOTES

NOTES